WHAT PEOPLE ARE SAYING ABOUT

MASTERING THE MOMMY TRACK

As a working mother of two young sons, and a professional woman passionate about my career AND my family, I recommend *Mastering the Mommy Track* for any working mom who feels the pressure to juggle it all. Work-life balance is something that each woman needs to find for herself, and no formula will fit everyone. This book does a wonderful job of talking about all the major sources of stress on a working mother and providing solutions that each individual mom can use in her own way to find a balance that works for her and her family. Whether you're becoming a mother for the first time, or well along the mommy track, you'll find this book to be a helpful guide through it all!

Sara Sutton Fell, the CEO and founder of FlexJobs.com

Erin Flynn Jay, who has been in this position herself, does an excellent job of helping moms learn to cope under the pressure of working in a down economy, when Dad's out of work or even not there at all. She gives the reader the benefit of opinions and advice from top experts in the field, and presents each problem in a helpful, organized format. An excellent resource for overwhelmed working moms.

Tina B. Tessina, PhD, (aka "Dr. Romance") psychotherapist and author of *Money, Sex and Kids: Stop Fighting about the Three Things That Can Ruin Your Marriage* www.tinatessina.com

As working moms, we are often running forward without taking a moment to think about our lives works best for ourselves, our family *Mommy Track* helps readers readjus

T0099169

back and contemplate the issues that impact us as working moms. It is difficult to find a way to create work-life synthesis, but not impossible. This book is a thoughtful resource that helps us identify the roadblocks and develop a plan, with the ultimate goals of having both a satisfying career and a family that feels they come first.

Allison O'Kelly, CEO of Mom Corps

Erin Flynn Jay covers the major concerns working moms with young kids face today, in a weak economy. Her timely book offers honest stories from mothers about their struggles and solutions from experts on how to overcome these issues. A self help guide on how to get through these uncertain times to achieve happiness at work and home.

Shannon Miller, Olympic gold medalist and mom

Mastering the Mommy Track

Juggling Career and Kids in Uncertain Times

Mastering the Mommy Track

Juggling Career and Kids in Uncertain Times

Erin Flynn Jay

BUSINESS BOOKS

Winchester, UK
Washington, USA

First published by Business Books, 2012
Business Books is an imprint of John Hunt Publishing Ltd., Laurel House, Station Approach,
Alresford, Hants, SO24 9JH, UK
office1@jhpbooks.net
www.johnhuntpublishing.com
www.jhpbusiness-books.com/

For distributor details and how to order please visit the 'Ordering' section on our website.

Text copyright: Erin Flynn Jay 2011

ISBN: 978 1 78099 123 8

A CIP catalogue record for this book is available from the British Library.

Design: Stuart Davies

Printed in the USA by Edwards Brothers Malloy

We operate a distinctive and ethical publishing philosophy in all
areas of our business, from our global network of authors to
production and worldwide distribution.

CONTENTS

Preface   1

Introduction   4

Part 1: Home Issues   7
1. Mental Health: I Am Overwhelmed – How Can I Cope?   8
2. Communication: How Can I Stop Fighting with
    My Spouse?   23
3. Finances: Are We on the Right Path?   41
4. Romance: Is It Still Possible?   56

Part 2: Health Issues   71
5. Sleep Deprivation: How Can I Cope with It?   72
6. Nutrition: How Do I Ensure My Family Eats Healthily?   87

Part 3: Parenting Issues   101
7. Parenting: How Do I Overcome Challenging Issues?   102
8. Childcare: What's the Best Solution?   118
9. Support: Who's My Care Network?   134

Part 4: Work-Life Issues   149
10 Time Management: How Can I Balance It All?   150
11. Self-Care: How Do I Find 'Alone' Time?   166
12. Work: Where Do I Take My Career?   180

Conclusion   193

Preface

This book tells the stories of everyday working mothers, recent challenges they have faced and lessons learned. It also offers solutions from experts on how mothers can overcome current issues in order to lead happy, healthy lives at home and work.

Many working mothers today face great tension between their families and careers and more financial pressure than ever. They are more likely than men to feel pressed for time and conflicted about being away from young children while working.

A 2010 Pew Research survey found that 30 months after it began, the Great Recession has led to a downsizing of Americans' expectations about their retirements and their children's future; a new frugality in their spending and borrowing habits; and a concern that it could take several years, at a minimum, for their house values and family finances to recover.

I felt called to write about this topic and 'followed my heart' to pursue it. When I first thought about covering it, my daughters were 1 year old and almost 3 years old. My husband Jason was out of work with no job prospects in sight, and we were experiencing some stress – financial and emotional.

As I conclude this book in February 2012, the downward mobility of the American middle class continues. Most of the new jobs being created are in the lower-wage sectors of the economy – hospital orderlies and nursing aides, secretaries and temporary workers, retail and restaurant, Salon.com reported. Millions of Americans who remain working agreed to cuts in wages and benefits. Others are settling for jobs that pay less than the jobs they've lost.

Other people are falling out of the middle class because they've lost their jobs, and many have also lost their homes. Almost one in three families with a mortgage is now underwater, holding their breath against imminent foreclosure, according to Salon.com.

The percent of Americans in poverty is its highest in two decades, and more of us are impoverished than at any time in the last 50 years. A recent analysis of federal data by the *New York Times* showed the number of children receiving subsidized lunches rose to 21 million in the last school year, up from 18 million in 2006 to 2007. Nearly a dozen states experienced increases of 25 percent or more. Under federal rules, children from families with incomes up to 130 percent of the poverty line, $29,055 for a family of four, are eligible.

Experts say the bad economy is the main factor driving the increase. According to an analysis of census data by the Center for Labor Market Studies at Northeastern University, 37 percent of young families with children were in poverty in 2010. That rate has likely worsened.

It is my hope career moms reading this book will take away insight that will help them improve all aspects of their lives – both personal and work related. It is a juggling act to balance home and work duties, and for a lot of women today, it's a walk on a tightrope – a fear their families will never experience the rewards (vacation, travel, time off) they so rightfully deserve.

I would like to thank my friends and family who supported me in writing this book. Special thanks to my mother Cathy who read many of the chapters and offered her opinion, and my brothers Dan and Brendan who read my blogs on this topic and provided feedback. My father Jim always offers uplifting words and guidance. Thanks to my husband Jason for watching the girls as needed so I could write and for cooking delicious meals.

I especially want to thank Timothy Staveteig, my literary agent and book editor. Tim helped me craft my idea into a proposal, first chapter and the final product. Tim's ongoing encouragement helped me see this book through until the end. Also, thank you to John Hunt, publisher of O Books, for taking a chance on me.

To my working mom contributors, thank you for honestly sharing your struggles and concerns. To my expert contributors, I appreciate your unique advice and knowledge. All of you helped me make this book a reality.

Thanks also to the Moms Club of Philadelphia board of which I am a member, and the Moonstone Preschool community (staff and parents). We are truly part of a supportive community in Philadelphia.

Introduction

What sparked your interest in this book? Perhaps the 'uncertain times'? So many mothers are now feeling an economic pinch. When I did research on this topic, I discovered a void in self-help books for women to get past these tough economic times. I decided to offer timely solutions for working mothers still reeling from the effects of the Great Recession.

The book is divided into four core sections: Home, Health, Parenting, and Work-Life. I designed my table of contents by jotting down 12 'trigger' areas I thought were of most concern to today's moms. I grouped those subjects into four areas.

Writing this was not a struggle for me as I love the topic. I'm a proud mommy – of course I love the topic! It was therapeutic to get my own personal thoughts down, and encouraging to meet many other moms dealing with the same issues. I did not mind writing during non-business hours or when the kids were asleep.

With this book, you'll be able to clearly identify areas of concern – lack of date nights with your spouse, no 'alone' time, or a need to switch careers to allow for 'my family' time, for example. The expert advice will be a good starting point for you to make immediate changes.

How you choose to implement these nuggets of advice is up to you. I hope this book – and others like it – will lead to more open discussions of what mothers are facing today and how they can get past their challenges.

As I noted, this book is divided into four parts. Home is the first section. Chapter 1 covers Mental Health – stories from everyday frazzled moms, and advice from psychologists on how mothers can keep their cool at home. Chapter 2 addresses Communication – career women who fought strongly with spouses after children were born, and insight from experts on how moms can best communicate with their spouses to avoid arguments or separations. Chapter 3 contains advice from financial experts on how couples can overcome financial hurdles, not skimp on items of importance and set a financial plan for the future. I address Romance in Chapter 4, which offers advice from experts on how women can keep the romance alive in their marriages when baby makes three.

Part 2 of this book is on Health – Sleep Deprivation and Nutrition. Chapter 5 contains interviews with mothers about their sleep issues and tips on how to overcome them. In Chapter 6, health experts weigh in on how time-pressed mothers can create nutrition plans for their families.

Parenting is the third section. Chapter 7 covers several challenging parenting issues and solutions to overcome them. Chapter 8 addresses childcare options available, and how you can determine the best plan for your family. Chapter 9 delves into Support – stories from moms on how they found support and how you can find it in your own community.

Part 4 of this book focuses on Work-Life issues. Chapter 10 on Time Management offers stories from working mothers on their time challenges and how they overcame them; work-life experts weigh in on how to best maximize your time. Chapter 11 delves into Self-Care, advice on how you can best care for yourself to avoid exhaustion and burnout. Chapter 12 closes on the topic of Work – stories of women who altered their careers to make more time for their families. Career experts also share tips on how mothers can take their careers to the next level – even with active home lives.

Part 1

Home Issues

Chapter 1

Mental Health: I Am Overwhelmed – How Can I Cope?

Being a new mom with an infant is one of the most challenging times in your life. You function on only a few hours of sleep each night and barely have time to shower. Then you return to work post-maternity leave, and you struggle with guilt for leaving your baby in someone else's hands.

When my first daughter Kaitlyn was born, I remember telling my husband Jason, 'This is the happiest day of my life.' It truly was. I was 36 when she was born, of 'advanced maternal age' as doctors would say. Fortunately, Jason and I were in agreement on wanting to have a baby shortly after we were married because of our older ages.

We were prepared for Kaitlyn's arrival – the crib and changing table were set up; baby clothes were in the drawers, breast pump and bottles ready, and so forth – but how do you mentally prepare for a baby's arrival? When Kaitlyn arrived, our lives changed for the better, but not without stress. A career mom, I wanted to return to work after a brief maternity leave but wondered how I would be able to juggle it all.

Shortly after my second daughter Emma was born, Jason lost his job. So in addition to the life change of having a baby, we dealt with another major life change – job loss.

Psychologists agree: working mothers are under tremendous pressure today, and the Great Recession has had an impact on their work and lifestyle. Stress that goes untreated can lead to serious illness such as cardiovascular disease. Mothers who feel ongoing and unresolved stress may develop significant medical illnesses or an anxiety disorder.

Chronic stress is a neuro-hormonal problem; it throws off

both your neurotransmitters and your stress hormones. 'These changes age you prematurely. The symptoms – poor stress resilience, brain fog, difficulty concentrating, fatigue, muffintops – are trying to tell us something. And with a rigorous strategy, they can be solved,' said Sara Gottfried, a Harvard-trained, board-certified integrative physician in Berkeley and author of *The Hormone Cure* (Scribner / Simon and Schuster, 2012).

Gottfried, since the economic downturn, is seeing in her medical practice dramatically increased stress, combined with poor stress resilience. 'Women feel like they are in survival mode. Stressed by affording their mortgage, stressed about job security. Of course, many of them have lost their jobs, especially older women over 45. Some of my patients lost their homes because of jumbo loans. Many are stressed by trying to afford to take care of their parents without burning themselves out completely,' she said.

Dr. Ella Lasky, a psychologist in private practice in Manhattan, therapist and parenting adviser, thinks the recession has impacted everyone. 'There are so few jobs out there that people are afraid to ask for any accommodations or special arrangements. I recently heard that a new mom was turned down when she asked to extend her maternity leave for several weeks without pay!' she said. Shocking, perhaps, but this is what is happening in many different companies.

In my experience, I have felt overwhelmed at times by the challenges of self-employment and raising two young daughters during tough economic times. I hear this from other working moms – they feel pressure to work, to constantly 'be on call' for their spouse and kids, and have trouble making time for themselves to relax. There is no easy solution.

Counter Incredible Stress by Focusing on the Now

Karol Ward, licensed clinical social worker and author of *Worried Sick: Break Free from Chronic Worry to Achieve Mental and Physical*

Health (Berkeley, 2010), shared what she has seen. 'The working moms I've had in my practice are incredibly stressed. Some of them have felt guilty for being employed while colleagues and friends have been laid off. Some of them have downplayed their successes so that they are not perceived as being 'high and mighty,' said Ward. 'Some of them are the primary breadwinners in their homes, and they need to work to keep their families afloat. They carry guilt for not being able to spend more time with their children even if their children are well cared for.'

There was a time earlier this year when I felt stress was seeping into my life and damaging my health. Jason was unemployed, and I lost my main PR client. I was concerned about our collective work prospects and how we could afford two daughters in daycare. I would awaken at night, go online, and search for new client opportunities.

Allison O'Kelly, CEO of Mom Corps, a national flexible staffing and search firm, shared her story of stress. 'Sanity amid chaos is a daily mantra in my house. I am the proud mother of three young boys, ages 8, 6, and two months. I am also the proud owner of a successful business that helps put moms like me to work across the country. But proud or not, some days, insanity gets the better of me,' she said.

In 2003, O'Kelly gave birth to her first son and decided to leave her corporate job at Toys 'R' Us to pursue the next phase of her life as a mother. She chose to keep her 'toe in the professional waters' by consulting as a CPA. Her mother had given her the advice to stay connected with the work world based on her own experience. Her mother had found herself on the job market after an 18-year absence when her husband (Allison's father) had unexpectedly died. Through play dates and playground conversations, O'Kelly was asked repeatedly how she managed to have both a career and time for the kids. This was a growing dilemma among mothers, and continues to be so.

The obstacles and challenges O'Kelly faced as a working

mother were the impetus for launching her company, Mom Corps. 'When it comes to helping stay-at-home moms return to the workforce after leaving to raise their kids, and helping others who need to find flexibility that they don't have in their current position, I know firsthand how difficult it is to juggle the two,' she said. 'My purpose is to find work for professionals that allows them to excel and best manage the stresses that come with being part of the workforce as a working mother.'

Never a dull moment in the O'Kelly household – around the time her third son was born, they learned that her husband had been transferred to Philadelphia for work and that they, or at least he, needed to move shortly. Two weeks after their son was born, her husband began work in Philadelphia, commuting to their home in Connecticut only on weekends. So, now added to O'Kelly's list of things to do was packing up the house and preparing it for sale in one of the worst housing markets in recent history.

O'Kelly has a small, but highly capable leadership team. As the sole proprietor, however, the proverbial buck stops with her. There is no maternity leave for a business owner. Familial demands cannot be left for another time. Everything happens simultaneously, every day.

'I don't think there are words to describe the utter stress and exhaustion that come from being a single weekday parent of three young boys while running a national business. I am used to working hard; I thrive in the element and am in control. With kids, there is no control,' she said. 'When it comes to time management and predictability, it is almost better if you period- ically let that go. There needs to be a part of your day when you just allow things to happen or else the pressure builds to unman- ageable proportions.'

O'Kelly finds her moments of peace when she lives in the moment – it works for her, for her kids and for her company. It's what allows her to enjoy all the aspects of her life. 'I'm not saying it's easy, quite the contrary. Every day, I assess what I can control and what I can't that day, and then move forward from there,' she added.

Living in the moment: this struck a chord with many women, including me. This is Mihály Csíkszentmihályi's flow state, but achieved not by reading a book or thinking about a problem, but getting focused on life right now. I also try to adhere to living in the moment. It's important to appreciate what is happening in your baby's or toddler's life each day. In the past, I have been guilty of focusing on tasks that needed to get done rather than simply enjoying small moments with my baby or toddler. I keep a to-do list of items and get frustrated when they aren't accomplished on time. I have often thought too much about future events rather than what was happening right in front of me.

Enjoy today – whether it be your baby's first steps or your two toddlers hugging and kissing each other. Let other things – such as items on your to-do list – wait. Breathe.

Avoid Alcohol or Drugs

With such intense pressure on career moms, many are turning to alcohol or drugs to calm frayed nerves. A November 2010 article in *Working Mother* magazine cites statistics that stress may drive more mothers to drink or abuse drugs. The article profiles women who suffer from alcohol and other addictions. Of those responding to the magazine survey, 40 percent say they drink to cope with stress, and 57 percent say they've misused prescription drugs.

The number of American women between the ages of 30 and 44 who abuse alcohol has doubled in the past ten years, and during the same period, prescription drug abuse has increased over 400 percent.

'Women today are under more stress than ever, and that stress can really go up if you're a working mom,' said Brenda Iliff, director of clinical services at Caron Treatment Centers in Dallas,

Texas. 'A working mom wears a lot of hats and may put her needs last. However, it's critical that she makes some time to take care of herself and find realistic and healthy ways of coping with her stress.'

Working moms turn to alcohol and drugs for various reasons. Some use alcohol or other drugs (including prescription) to deal with depression and anxiety or pain issues, cope with stress, reward themselves, boost energy, or kick-start weight loss, to name the major reasons.

According to Iliff, some of the signs that you may have a problem with alcohol or drugs include:

- Your value system starts to change. You used to allow yourself a girls' night out once a week – but now you're going out three times a week regularly and your kids are obviously upset, but you cannot stop.
- You make promises both at work and at home that you cannot keep.
- Your friends and loved ones start to express concerns about your behavior.
- You start to make excuses to your job that your child is sick – when in reality you cannot make it in because you're hung over.
- You are isolating yourself from important others more frequently.

What can working moms do if they think they have a problem?

- Don't try to 'fix' the problem by yourself. 'For high-functioning moms, this can bring about great feelings of shame, but it's important for moms to know they are not alone,' Iliff said. 'There are many moms who have had problems with chemicals and have asked for help to deal with it.'

- Get your behavior assessed. If it turns out you have the disease of addiction, get or accept immediate intervention and treatment. Iliff said it's not a character flaw or moral failing.

What can you do if you think a working mom friend or family member has a problem? Iliff suggested:

- Get involved. It's important to say something, but also important to know when to say something. Talk about it, but not when the person is under the influence or immediately after a crisis, Iliff said.
- Share your concern with the behavior you are observing. How has it changed? How does it impact others?
- Offer options to her. Check out what might be some helpful places to get an assessment or other helpful resources and offer possibly to go with her.
- Set boundaries or limits on what you will or will not do. 'I will call the police if I see you driving while smelling of alcohol again with the children in the car,' and be willing to follow through.
- Keep the children's safety at the top of the list. There may be a time to get other help involved.

Addiction is a chronic disease. If left untreated, it can have devastating and even fatal consequences. Seek professional help or express concerns about a person you care about before it's too late.

Facing Addiction

Gottfried shared her own story of addiction. She wasn't always a Zen yoga teaching, integrative physician, and book-writing mom. Her husband reminded her recently of a typical post-workday pattern ten years ago: 'You'd come home from work with a grim look, say a curt "hello" to me and the kids, go upstairs to draw your hot bath, and pour yourself a generous glass of red wine.'

Gottfried lived the mantra of the modern women: she overworked, overate, over-drank, overachieved, over-exercised, over-delivered, over-gave. Until she couldn't anymore. 'I was working at an HMO seeing 30 patients per day and observing my authenticity slowly drain out of me. I kept showing up for work because of the security and benefits, until I couldn't anymore,' she confessed. 'Until I realized true security is much deeper, and connects to your inner pilot light. My inner pilot light was barely on. I was burned out. I knew I had to change my work life.'

She hired a coach and planned an 18-month escape hatch from the HMO to her own integrative medicine practice for women. Gottfried opened her practice, and it was wildly successful. She quickly filled her appointments out for six months. Then she realized that she was burning herself out in an entirely new way. The patient she most needed to heal was herself.

After having two kids and learning to be an entrepreneur, she tested her adrenal hormones, and found these stress indicators were extremely high all day long. She began 'Mission Ignition: Heal Dr. Sara's Adrenals.'

After many years of trial and error, Gottfried figured aspects out about herself (and the same applies to many of her patients) including:

1   Find proportion, rather than balance. Balance is elusive: balanced hormones, work-life balance, couple time vs. family time. Now Gottfried chooses proportion. One of the most important ways to stay in proportion is to notice how much time you spend in the sympathetic side of your nervous system – the so-called 'fight or flight' syndrome, where stress, high blood pressure and fast heart rate

dominates. Counter it with time in your parasympathetic nervous system, or 'rest and digest' state. You can increase your time spent in parasympathetic tone with slow, mindful eating, slow, mindful breathing, and slow, mindful sex. It's amazing how good sex balances your cortisol, the main hormone of stress.

2 Regular, long vacations. Affording them is a reach, but retreating at least two weeks every summer and again at the winter school break is essential. Not taking a generous vacation is outrageously expensive for Gottfried's adrenal glands. During vacation: digital sabbatical. No iPhone, no email checking, no availability.

Living Solo with an Infant

Amy Smith (name changed), a working mother based in Manhattan, shared her challenging story as a single mom with a ten-week old boy. Smith was previously running a small communications firm in NYC with her business partner. She became engaged in fall 2010, got pregnant, and moved to another country to be with her fiancé and his family. He is now her ex-fiancé. 'Our engagement ended two months before I gave birth. I moved back to NYC in the dead of winter to a company winding down. I had one mini suitcase – all of my belongings were still in the other country. Talk about stress!' she confided.

Smith has since given birth, moved, and began a new path with her infant and a job at a major network. Childcare is still an issue as she has not found the right person, but most likely she is going to hire an au pair. 'I have had to fight through the most vulnerable time in my life,' she divulged. 'I'm educated and have a great family, but I've learned that no one is immune to life's downfalls.'

With her son only ten weeks old, it's challenging for Smith to start all over. She is trying to figure this out day by day, and it's a process. 'I have to find the best care for my son so I can focus on making a living for both of us; I have family right now to help out,' Smith said. 'I do not want to leave him in the hands of a stranger. I am concerned also about having to get home from a job at a certain time – it puts more stress on me. I may have to try a completely different career path altogether that allows me more flexibility.'

So Smith is concerned about finding quality childcare for her son so she can work and support them. She is also concerned about the career implications of having to leave her job at a set time on weekdays to return to her son. It's a stressful time for her, compounded by the fact she has to make major decisions on her own.

Here is some advice for Smith and many mothers in this situation.

Evaluate the situation over time:

Ward advises her clients to do a few things to cope if they have an economic situation that is not changing for a while.

1 Use one-, two- or six-month time periods, and at the end of them, take stock of how things are working and if not, what needs to change.

2 Stay out of your head. 'Worry and stress do not create rational thinking. I tell the working moms to use the power of observation to keep on track. If their kids are happy and thriving, and their significant other is content, then things are probably fine,' she said.

Unwind before arriving home:

1 One tip that many of Lasky's patients have appreciated over the years is to take an extra ten minutes on the way home – sit down somewhere for ten relaxing minutes. 'You can experiment with how many minutes you, as an individual, actually need. You can experiment with relax-

ation breathing, listening to music, reading something not work or family related. The goal is to clear your head of work and get ready to enjoy your family. Simple, but effective!' Lasky said.

2   Most moms go from one situation to another without any breathing time. When you can, build in some space between work and home. 'These could be things like putting in some form of movement before you walk in the door such as a walk or exercise class; finding a quiet place to sit without working for even 15 minutes such as your desk, your car, a coffee shop or park; or keeping any help such as a sitter or husband in place while Mom goes to her room to lie down, stretch, read or listen to music while the kids play outside or are engaged in an activity,' Ward said.

Dispel First-Baby Pressures

Amy Przeworski, assistant professor of psychology at Case Western University, returned to work after 14 weeks of maternity leave. 'It was difficult to go from working in a high-pressure position to giving birth and suddenly spending most of my time with an infant. It was also tough to be recovering from having had a C-section, but having virtually no time to sleep or to take care of my own needs. I can remember being afraid that I might not have time to eat for several hours if my daughter was awake and having a hard time,' Przeworski said. *'This was also my first child* so I felt like I had no idea what I was doing and was struggling to transition from being a somewhat independent, career-focused woman to becoming a temporary stay-at-home mom.'

In a tenure-track position, Przeworski was also attempting to publish and put in several hours of work every day from home. 'It was really difficult to balance my daughter's needs, my own needs, and what I thought I needed to be doing in order to succeed in my career. I can remember many times when I felt like I was failing at all of it,' Przeworski said. 'I still feel that way sometimes. My mom was a stay-at-home mom so I had no model for how to balance all of this and felt really lost in the beginning.'

I can relate to Przeworski's struggles. I also felt it was tough to balance my daughters' needs when they were babies and my own. With both girls, I returned to work after a six-week maternity leave. When you are self-employed, no paid maternity leave is available, and I did not want too much time to lapse away from clients. I would get my work done when the baby was down for naps or hire a sitter when I had assignments at the computer. I would set conference calls when I knew baby would be asleep, but sometimes things did not always go according to plan.

Przeworski's stress was high back then and still is high, but it has changed. 'Back then, I struggled with what I thought were competing roles – me as a mom, me as a career woman, me as a wife, me as a daughter. It was easy to feel overwhelmed by all of the roles. Now I see them all as integrated,' she said. 'I am C's mom, the one who comforts her when she is upset about something and the one whom she loves to kiss. I am also an assistant professor on the tenure track, a mentor to students, a wife, a daughter, and all of those things are intertwined in me rather than being separate versions of me.'

Przeworski thinks it is incredibly difficult to be a professional woman and balance your career with housework and being a mom. 'Women still do the lion's share of housework, and I often feel pressure to be the perfect homemaker, career woman, and mom,' she admitted.

Przeworski's daughter has been in daycare four days a week since she returned to work. She tried to work from home one day a week to make sure she maintained a connection to her daughter and didn't feel like she was entirely missing her daughter's infancy while at work. 'She will be at daycare five days a week now (at ten months of age), and she is at a daycare where she is very happy. That made the transition of going back to work much easier. In fact, I felt more like "me" once I was back at work, doing what I always loved during the day and going home to my beautiful little girl at night,' Przeworski said.

Her job is flexible, and she can often work from home if she needs to. 'That is fantastic, but can also lead to some bleeding between my home life and my work life. I often work between the hours of 7:30 p.m. and 11 p.m., but may take some time off between 4 p.m. and 7:30 p.m. to see her. I can stay at home with her if she's sick, as long as I'm not teaching and don't have meetings scheduled that day,' Przeworski said. 'But I have to make sure that I continue to meet my goals and therefore end up working from home a lot on weekends and evenings which someone with a more structured schedule may have entirely off.'

This applies to me as well. I often work evenings and weekends to meet deadlines and catch up on projects. I love having a flexible schedule during the week. This allows me to pick up my daughters from daycare at 3 p.m. and then take them to the park or for a play date. The disadvantage is that I don't get a lot of free time at night after I put the kids to bed because I often have to return to 'the office.'

Przeworski admitted, 'My psychology background helped in some ways, but parenting is still the most difficult thing that I think a person can do. It is much harder to be a parent than it is to tell other parents how to parent. My psychology background also helped me to be aware of the links between infant temperament and later outcomes, and even the importance of parent psychological health in terms of the baby's health (mental and physical). That helped me to handle some of the difficulties that are inherent in parenting.'

Keeping Cool at Home

Based on my interviews with psychologists, here are some tips to help you keep your cool at home:

- *Slow down after work.* Spend some time with your children, even if it is just 20 minutes before you get dinner prepared and cooked. Appreciate the small moments you have.
- *Set the proper example.* Children look up to parents and follow their role. Make sure you aren't yelling at your kids over spilling snacks or drawing on the wall.
- *Give yourself some credit.* Commend yourself for getting through each hectic day. No one is perfect. You won't get every project finished on time. Do your best each day and realize the rest will have to wait until tomorrow. Don't be too tough on yourself – it's okay to make mistakes. Let your children know it's okay for them to also make mistakes.
- *Communicate your needs to others.* Let your spouse or partner, family members, and friends know what you need. This could be asking that groceries be purchased and put away, dinner be started, toys picked up, laundry folded, and so forth. Instead of reacting to unmet needs, moms can be proactive by expressing their needs from the start. When your needs are met, there is less exasperation.
- *Set a weekly family meeting.* Before the start of the next work/school week, gather the family together to discuss the upcoming week. This should not be a mealtime, where there are easily distractions. Everyone should get a chance to speak about upcoming events, projects or situations.

In conclusion, career moms should realize that the economic downturn is nationwide; millions of others are experiencing the hardships your family is. The events happening today will turn around in the future. Your spouse will get a job in his field again; it just may take more time. You will land new clients if you keep up the prospecting efforts.

Strive to be a good enough mother and not a perfect mother. As I stated earlier, perfection is impossible. Do the best you can for your children, yourself and your partner. Too many women fall into the 'perfect mother' trap where they expect to accomplish their goals immediately. It doesn't happen that way. Take one day at a time, and make each day as special and productive as possible.

Chapter 2

Communication: How Can I Stop Fighting with My Spouse?

The baby arrives, and life suddenly gets more stressful for you and your husband. You are trying to function on only a few hours of sleep each night, breastfeeding on demand. Your husband does not want to change messy baby diapers or outfits. You race from one task to another, somewhat resentful he is not helping out more.

Sound familiar? If you were making a list of your concerns in a journal, smart phone or mental record, what would you list? What are the themes of this 'life with baby' stress? Was communication one of your items? If not, then examine your list again because the solution to each frustration is to talk about it. After my second child's birth, I learned of the deep need for this.

The Usual Suspects

When speaking with working women, I heard several themes mentioned over and again: money burdens or concerns, work pressures, infrequent companionship, and childcare responsibilities (or apportionment of household duties). This rings true with Dr. Tina B. Tessina's research in her book, *Money, Sex and Kids* (Adams Media, 2008). After the kids arrive, spouses *clash* about sharing the work, parenting, or money concerns. In fact, Dr. Tessina uses the word *fight*, which may not be too strong for many relationships.

Dr. Michelle P. Maidenberg, clinical director of Westchester Group Works, said spouses struggle (or fight) about the following after the kids arrive:

1   The restructuring of roles: Who will accomplish household

responsibilities, child-rearing, maintain the finances, and so forth?

2 Finances: How will you earn your income, what will you spend it on, and how much will you spend?

3 Time-management issues: How much time should you spend with one another, with and without the children?

4 General childcare issues: How will you handle discipline, child-rearing, childcare, and so forth?

5 Intimacy: What are your sexual intimacy, emotional closeness and support, and similar needs? How will these be fulfilled for you and your spouse?

Based on my interviews with career moms, the main communication issues I uncovered between spouses or partners seem to focus on (1) the sharing of household duties, (2) finances, and (3) time management.

The Great Recession's Impact

The Great Recession and its aftershocks certainly agitated my family's life as well as some other family members. I was curious to know if the recession has impacted other couples negatively, and if so – how?

The women with whom I talked surely felt the Great Recession affected them negatively. When corporate profitability rebounded in 2011 to pre-recession levels, it did so with 2.5 million fewer workers. Many women considered themselves the sole breadwinner as their careers stayed on track, while their spouses were out of work for lengthy periods of time. Some women, however, were facing longer work hours, no pay raises, and a sense they needed to work at a full-time job in order to keep family healthcare benefits.

Another group of women has largely been ignored, namely, those who are self-employed. Just as my small business faced declining revenues, my husband lost his job. It was a stressful experience for us, especially since we have two young children. The stress has subsided a bit as we learned to cope with the situation and work together as a team to overcome daily issues. I knew, however, that a better way than trial-and-error must exist.

Dr. Maidenberg thinks the recession has hurt couples: 'There tends to be more financial stressors which cause overall stress within the couple dynamic.' Examples could include greater dissatisfaction because:

1 Fewer opportunities for job advancement, changing, or transferring jobs are available
2 Not being financially able to hire a babysitter means less 'couple time'
3 Fewer family and couple vacations decreases ability to 'de-stress'
4 Appropriation of daily overall spending can lead to vigorous debates
5 The family cannot achieve increased comfort through, for example, home renovations
6 General fear or concern about the future surrounds life at home

Dr. Tessina acknowledged that such discomfort depends on the couple. 'Some people, those who have hung onto their jobs, not over-mortgaged their homes, etc., are doing okay. Others are feeling the pinch, and the stress increases argument time,' she said. 'If a couple really overspends, with no savings, they can lose their home, which becomes the source of a lot of blaming and fighting. Healthy couples will work together to handle financial ups and downs.'

So at least some women could be facing not only a tight budget but also economic ruin. And all women may have this specter in mind. A couple's relationship is vulnerable whenever the couple experiences financial distress. Communication patterns, already in place, are tested by the couple's physical or financial circumstances.

Transition to Parenthood

If the issues and anxieties seem rather consistent among couples, then the solutions or strategies are less so. In this chapter, I share stories from mothers who have fought strongly with their partners or spouses after the baby was born. I also offer advice from experts on how working mothers can keep the peace with their significant others.

Robyn Hauptman is a human resource manager in Philadelphia. Married five years now, she was married three years when her son was stillborn and then four years when her daughter was born. 'I was really surprised about how much my husband and I fought after my baby was born. We had been through so much, and it never dawned on me how we would both struggle with transitioning to parenthood,' Hauptman told me. 'Our first child was stillborn. We really cared for each other so well after that happened, and it was like we forgot how to do that when my daughter arrived. It really got bad... and finally one day I was listening to Dr. Laura. While she would very much disagree with the fact that I work, she reminded me that it was not ever an option to separate from my husband. Once I made that my mantra, I was able to step out of my stuff and act more compassionately toward my husband.'

Hauptman went back to work when her daughter was four months old. 'I had a very difficult time transitioning to having a newborn. My daughter is now 14 months, and I am just starting to get the hang of things. It has taken that long to want to be a wife again,' she said. 'I think that is what was so hard. I just felt like initially there was only enough of me to be a mom, and I really was not interested in being a wife. I know that sounds so horrible and thank goodness I do not feel that way anymore. Who knows, maybe it was hormones or grief from losing our first baby, but boy I was unprepared for all of the emotion that follows giving birth.'

Many other new mothers expressed similar themes. The first few months with baby were extremely difficult. Many mothers went back to work after a (too) brief maternity leave. Home life got much easier when their children turned 1 year old. Then, mother and child had developed a routine. The child, for example, would sleep until 7 a.m. so that the mother got more rest. Many also expressed relief when their child was weaned, and breastfeeding ended, because it was such a time commitment and physically draining as well.

These same mothers struggle with the transition to parenthood – lack of sleep, new responsibilities, less time for self, hormones out of sync, and so on. This can easily result in disagreements with your spouse or partner, and issues, if not addressed, can simmer and suddenly boil over or get heated.

Hauptman said she and her husband argued about everything. 'First, it was about me going back to work, vaccines, sleep, you name it. We have resolved almost all issues.' Hauptman's husband is self-employed as a healthcare professional. 'We have kept our heads above water, but I still need to work. It is just a lot of pressure owning our own business, keeping up at my job, and mostly making every moment with our daughter count.'

Sole Household Earners

The percentage of women who have children under 6 years of age and who are working has nearly doubled since 1975 (from 40 percent to over 70 percent in 2009, according to US Department of Labor Bureau of Labor Statistics). For many women, their income is needed to carry about one-half of the financial burden. Yet, more than a few women are the sole earners for their households.

Sabrina Mizrachi, a lawyer at a big firm in Philadelphia, also argued with her husband heavily in the past. Fortunately, home life is better now. 'I finally got my husband to stop arguing with me by completely melting down and begging him to communicate properly with me. I also became more quiet so that I don't take my stress out on him. When I went back to work four months after my baby was born, my husband stopped working and went to graduate school for a masters in education. He's almost done with his program (one class remains to be completed), but doesn't have a job yet. So I'm a working mom and the sole earner in my household,' Mizrachi told me. 'I've been back at work for 22 months, and it hasn't gotten any easier at all to be away from my son – in fact, it's gotten harder. (I travel a lot, averaging about three trips a month.)'

So Mizrachi is facing pressure to be the sole financial provider, achieve a healthy work-life balance, and overcome stress because she is missing time spent with her son. Based on advice I gleaned, here is a solution for Mizrachi:

1 *Have a weekly discussion.* This is not an argument or complaint session, but an opportunity to update each other on how things are going between you. 'I recommend it because stressed couples often tend to avoid talking about what's going on until a problem is created [or uncovered]. If you keep each other informed of both the good things and the problems on a regular basis, nothing will get out of hand or become too dramatic to solve easily,' Tessina said. 'This works every time with every couple in counseling with me who are willing to do it.'

2 *Accentuate the positive.* 'When you speak, always start out by accentuating the positive and reinforcing his positive behaviors and attributes – he will be more open and inclined to listen to you,' Maidenberg said. 'Talk specifically about his observations and behaviors, and detail specific changes you want to see being made. Convey a

trusting, caring, and empathetic tone so that your husband will be more inclined to want to express himself – and will feel that you care about his feelings/needs as well.'

Be conscious of when you speak to your husband. 'Express yourself when there is opportunity to have dialogue, not when you're half listening and trying to manage sibling conflict at the same time,' Maidenberg added. 'Be sure that your desires or requests are realistic, feasible, and manageable; check in to see how your husband feels about these new changes in the way he used to accomplish things.'

3   *Express love.* 'Be a positive role model – be conscious of all the things you are asking your husband to pay attention to – that is, practice what you preach. No one appreciates a double standard,' Maidenberg said. 'Make sure to always give compliments and express appreciation when it is due. Your husband is a well-intended person and deserves to hear this so that the times when you are asking for things or negotiating with him won't seem so daunting.'

The relationships depicted in the media (and perhaps your own parents' relationship) do not model kind, loving, and considerate behavior very well. 'Although the press may be bored by politeness, kindness, and happiness, those traits will make your partner – and your relationship – flourish and blossom. Consider kindness to be the lubricant of your communication and expressing love to be the fertilizer that makes the relationship bloom,' Tessina said.

4   *Care for yourself and your partner.* 'Guard against sacrificing too much by making sure you care about yourself in four areas: emotionally, mentally, physically, and spiritually. Guard against narcissism and selfishness by caring about your partner in the same four areas,' Tessina said. 'Achieving balance in these areas is the best way to ensure

that your relationship will thrive, and no one will carry too much resentment, which is the only emotion that can destroy love.'

Caring for Each Other

Caring for each other is critical. Unfortunately, many couples with babies fall into the pattern of attacking each other as they don't know effective coping methods for dealing with the stress. It's not healthy to treat each other viciously. If you find your relationship is getting volatile, then it's time to follow this advice or, better yet, talk to an outside counselor or therapist.

I was fortunate to have been raised by two exemplary parents who never fought in front of my brothers and me, and who expressed nothing but love and care for each other and their children. My parents have been married 40 years now; they still love each other deeply and have great relationships with myself and my brothers.

Jason and I do fight at times and sometimes disagree on important issues. The past year and a half has been especially trying for us as we have each faced career challenges.

I can also relate to Mizrachi's experience, as I was the sole household earner when Jason was out of work. I feel fortunate I don't have to do any lengthy travel – just local face-to-face meetings from time to time. Jason was unemployed for over a year. We had a good home routine down, and Jason was helpful with providing childcare as needed and cooking dinner (he's a gourmet cook). But he, like other fathers hit by this tough economy, is concerned about when he will find a suitable opportunity in his field of finance, and if it will be enough to meet our family's needs. I strive to run a successful business from our home, one that will generate enough income to exceed our family's expenses and meet our daughters' future education costs.

I have also been concerned about when Jason will find the

right job opportunity. When so much time passes and a spouse remains unemployed, you begin to question how hard they are looking for work. I heard this complaint from other women with unemployed spouses – it was a source of great strife in their relationships.

Krista Blaisdell is a single mother in Las Vegas, Nevada, who never married her daughter's father. She works full-time as a senior account executive for a public relations/public affairs firm. 'My daughter's father and I fight about household and child-rearing responsibilities. I realize now this is because the Women's Movement only gave us the right to have a career. It didn't provide any additional support at home,' Blaisdell told me with a laugh. 'I often think I just have to accept this and hope it's better when my daughter grows up. At the same time, I want her to see her dad participate in housework and cooking so she chooses a partner who will help with those tasks.'

The argument they keep having is about child-related responsibilities – mainly household and financial. This issue has not been resolved. 'It's always an ongoing argument that pops up when I'm particularly exhausted or stressed out,' she said.

Evaluate Your Communication

No matter what you're fighting about – money, sex, kids or something else – the fighting is an indication that your communication isn't working. 'If this happens only occasionally, such as when one or both of you are tired or stressed, it's not too big a problem. However, if you argue or bicker on a daily (or even weekly) basis, or you keep fighting about the same thing over and over, then your communication is not functioning as it should, and you don't know how to move from a problem to the solution,' Tessina said. 'When this happens, problems are recurrent, endless, and can be exaggerated into relationship disasters.'

Childcare responsibilities are one of the major issues for

working parents, and both partners need to participate in order for there to be harmony at home. Here is a solution for Blaisdell's communication gap:

1. *Organize your thoughts before speaking:* 'When speaking with him, speak his language – if he intellectualizes, speak from an intellectual point of view; if he tends to get defensive, know the things that get him defensive and talk to him sensitively about those topics,' Maidenberg said. 'Practice what you are going to say, and think of your husband as a friend and someone who cares about you and wants the best for you, as opposed to being the enemy.'

   Make sure you and your partner understand each other's point of view before beginning to solve the problem. 'You should be able to put your mate's position in your own words, and vice versa. This does not mean that you agree with each other, just that you understand each other,' Tessina said.

2. *Be specific:* Speak clearly, avoid using jargon, and be specific about what you are referring to. 'Use "I" statements, not accusatory "you" statements, which convey judgment and disapproval. A "you" statement doesn't communicate a feeling but conveys a belief about the other person. He will be less likely to listen/hear what you are saying,' Maidenberg advised. 'Use the four parts of the "I" statement when you are communicating: (a) "When you ..., (b) the effects are ..., (c) I feel ..., and (d) I'd prefer it if ...." For example, "Whenever you show up at the house when it's the children's bedtime, [the effects are that] it makes it a more difficult process to get them to bed on time so that they wake up alert the next day for school. [I feel] I would really appreciate enjoying your company if you came home at a time when the kids and I can enjoy you. I would really prefer it if you let me know in advance when you will be

home so I can plan things accordingly.'

3. *Discuss recurring problems:* To resolve recurring problems, Tessina advises you to discuss related decisions with your spouse and find out what each of you does and does not want before making important decisions. You have a lot of options; don't let confusion add to the stress. 'Remember, always address whatever you are unhappy with early – before it builds up inside and you are more likely to raise your voice, express yourself with judgment and anger, and are less likely to listen to what he has to say,' Maidenberg said.

4. *Don't participate:* Disagreements always require two people. 'If you don't participate, your partner can't argue without you. If the issue arises at an inopportune time, then you can just find a temporary resolution (temporarily give in, go home, leave the restaurant) and wait until things calm down to discuss what happened – the squabble may just have been a case of too much alcohol, or being tired and irritable,' Tessina said. 'Then talk about what you can do instead if it ever happens again.'

Squabbles often occur because you're following automatic habit patterns that lead to a problem before you know it. Using these guidelines will help you speak his language and overcome negative habit patterns you may have built that lead to arguments or bickering.

I agree wholeheartedly that it's important not to argue in front of the kids. No matter how mad you are, just walk away, cool down, and take up the conversation later when the kids are asleep and you are both calmer.

Blaisdell's issue is a common one. Many of the mothers I spoke to thought their husbands or partners should pick up more of the domestic duties. The era when most women would stay at home to manage the household ('home economics') is over. Currently, seven out of ten women with children are in the labor force.

Role Confliction

The majority of Americans (75 percent) think that women should not return to their traditional roles in society, and most believe that both husband and wife should contribute to the family income. In spite of these attitude changes, many women remain conflicted about the dual roles they play at work and home. Working mothers are uncertain about whether full-time work is the best thing for them or their children; they feel the pull of family much more strongly than working fathers do. As a result, most working mothers find themselves in a situation that they think is less than ideal.

They are also more likely than either at-home moms or working dads to feel as if there just is not enough time in the day. According to the Pew Research Center, four in ten say they always feel hurried, compared with a quarter of the other two groups. But despite these pressures, working moms are as likely as at-home moms and working dads to say they are happy with their lives.

Whether women work outside the home or not, family responsibilities have a clear impact on the key life choices they make. Roughly three in ten women who are not currently employed (27 percent) say family duties keep them from working. And family appears to be one of the key reasons that many do not break through the 'glass ceiling' to the top ranks of management – at least, that is the view of about a third of the public. These are interesting figures from the Pew Research Center, and identify the impact family responsibilities have on women today.

Further, a 2010 Procter and Gamble survey of more than 1,000 American fathers revealed that 91 percent of dads feel their relationship with their significant other is better when they share household chores equally. The online survey, conducted by Kelton Research, uncovers how fathers see their relationships improve as a result of that contribution. So, if fathers assisted more with household tasks, then their spouses or partners would be happier, and their relationships would improve for the better.

Another communication issue for Blaisdell is money. 'My daughter's father hates to talk about money – even a reasonable conversation irritates him. In truth, I don't think he has any idea of a total cost per month spent on our daughter. I don't say anything until I'm so annoyed I blow up, which doesn't help the communication process at all.'

The recession has affected her negatively. 'I haven't had a pay raise in the past three years. Because business is down, I no longer receive quarterly cash bonuses to supplement my income. My daughter's father was laid off from his job (which meant no cash from him during that time), but has since found work.' Many ex-spouses are good about paying child support when they have jobs. A period of unemployment, however, can mean a gap in income for child and mother.

Many of the women I spoke with said they often fought with their significant other about money, and the economic downturn had a negative impact on their household income. More than half (55 percent) of all adults in the labor force say that since the Great Recession began in 2008, they have suffered a spell of unemployment, a cut in pay, a reduction in hours, or have become involuntary part-time workers, according to a June 2010 survey by the Pew Research Center's Social and Demographic Trends Project.

The survey also found that the recession has led to a new frugality in Americans' spending and borrowing habits; a diminished set of expectations about their retirements and their children's future; and a concern that it will take several years, at a minimum, for their family finances and house values to recover.

Job Salaries Are Critical

Kelly Conrad, based in Southern California, balances doing public relations for over 40 wine brands, working weekends, and traveling – with a family of 4. 'My kids are 6 and 2, and my husband is a special education teacher at the local high school. We seem to have the same arguments over and over about how "I think my job is more important than my family," which is, of course, not true, but my job pays more, and therefore I feel pressure to perform well and keep this job since a teacher's salary would not cover our mortgage and cost of living.'

I discovered this issue from some of the other mothers as well. These women had jobs that may not have been their ideal jobs, but they did not want to give them up because they considered their salaries and benefits decent, if not excellent.

Conrad told me with her and her husband's first child, their arguments were more about parenting styles: Do we let her cry it out? Do we force naps or just put her down early? Who takes the night shift? 'Before our second child was born, we had settled most of those arguments. But then our fights started to be more about not being lackadaisical in our parenting style and about money, since I wasn't earning as much on maternity leave. He was a stay-at-home dad for a while and that also sparked many money fights, which at the core were him just feeling doubt about his contribution to the family since he wasn't bringing home a paycheck,' she said.

Because hormones were running rampant, and because the introduction of babies was a joyful but stressful time, Conrad said it was easy to let arguments fly out of control; they quickly lost track of what they were arguing about, and things got personal, even at times vicious. The core of most of their arguments was who was carrying more weight. 'I would feel I was doing more because I would work, and then, when I came home, I would be instantly "on" again as mom, bathing the kids, doing the night routine, and so on,' Conrad said. 'He would feel like he was doing more because he would teach school, and be "on" as dad for three hours until I got home. During this period, he would do the cooking and other household chores as well as watch the children. It took us a while to pull our heads out of our own little worlds to see that we were both working hard for our family and that we needn't keep tabs or a score sheet.'

Conrad said these arguments have been resolved. The lesson she learned? 'Sometimes just a break away from the routine and each other is all you need to gain a fresh perspective on things,' she said.

Conrad's suggestion is a good one. If you feel stressed or burned out, tell your husband you need to get out of the house alone for an hour or two, and ask him to take care of the kids. I do this on occasion, and Jason does it as well. Sometimes fresh air and a good walk are all you need to refocus.

Communication Guidelines

The working mothers I interviewed honestly shared their communication struggles with me as well as their strategies for overcoming such struggles. Some of these worked better than others. So how can women best communicate with their spouses or partners to avoid arguments or separations?

Here are some ways to avoid arguments with your significant other:

- *Solve it for the two of you:* Come up with a solution that works for just the two of you, ignoring anyone else's needs. 'It's much easier to solve a problem for the two of you than for others you may not understand. After you are clear with each other, discuss the issues with others who may be involved,' Tessina said.
- *Talk to others:* If extended family members or friends might have problems with your decision, Tessina said to talk about what objections they might have, so you can diffuse

them beforehand. Discuss possible ways to handle their objections.

This pointer was beneficial to me as there are many relatives involved in our kids' lives. Jason and I have discussed issues and diffused them. Remember, you and your husband are the parents. Extended family members might not agree with a decision you make, but ultimately you're in charge.

I like to tell Jason immediately if I am unhappy about something rather than let it fester and brew. I think that technique has helped us avoid some arguments.

Remember, you and your significant other are working together to raise healthy children and instill in them proper values. You both need to set the right example. I remember being told as a child, 'Always treat others as you would like to be treated.' I will teach my own two daughters to do the same.

How often do you argue with your spouse or partner? Fighting is an indication that your communication isn't working. If this happens occasionally, it's not a major concern. But if you argue or bicker on a daily (or weekly) basis, then communication is not functioning as it should, and you need to solve the recurrent problem. If not addressed, disagreements can spiral downwards and – in some cases – lead to separation or divorce.

Trigger Areas

Examine the following areas which may lead to frustration or differences:

1 Household responsibilities: Is your spouse participating in his fair share of household tasks? I've spoken to many mothers who assume control of food shopping, cooking, cleaning, baby care, and so forth – they feel their husbands are not assisting enough. How hands-on is your spouse or partner with the baby? If he does not want to change baby

diapers, then remind him you are in an equal partnership and he needs to do this – no task should be hands-off. Talk with your partner about your frustrations and tell him you need him to help out more in certain areas. Be specific: 'If you can assume the weekend grocery shopping and cook dinner tonight, that would be a tremendous help.'

2 Finances: Discuss how you each will earn your income, your projected salaries, and how you plan to spend or save this; review major expenses. Can both salaries cover your expenses? If not, what are you prepared to do to change that? Perhaps one of you should go after a higher-paying job or your husband should open up that side business or you should consider lowering your expenses. You could sell your house and buy a more affordable one. You get the idea – all options should be explored so you can stay financially sound.

Also, have an honest discussion about what you each spend your money on and how much you spend. There should be no surprises. If your husband gambles at a casino weekly or hits the neighborhood bar five nights a week, then you should know about it. If you have a joint checking account, keep tabs on that – if an excessive amount is withdrawn, ask your husband what he took this money out for.

3 Time-management issues: How much time do you spend with the kids? How much time do you spend with each other? I like to take my girls outside as much as possible, but sometimes just need a breather from them. I'll ask Jason to take them out for a few hours if I need a break. I may say to him, 'I had the kids all day yesterday, so would like tomorrow afternoon to myself.' Let your husband know when you need more alone time on the weekends.

Also, make sure you and your spouse are spending some quality time alone together. Many couples allot certain nights 'Date Night' when they get a babysitter and go out for dinner or a movie. If your babysitter is too expensive or if hiring a babysitter is an issue, then find one who will babysit at a cheaper rate, or trade duties with another couple. It's critical you both get out and do non-kid-related activities.

4   Childcare issues: Discuss the age your children will start daycare and where they will go, who will babysit as needed, and a discipline strategy, among other child-rearing aspects. As you raise your children, communicate your concerns and listen to your spouse's feedback. Issues will arise that you will have to address and come to an agreement on.

What Conrad mentioned earlier is key – you don't want to keep a scorecard of who does what. Realize you're both working hard for your family. But if you feel your husband needs to step up in a certain area, then let him know, and listen to his response. There may be times when one of you will have to handle more family tasks than the other – if your spouse is ill or working longer hours, for example.

Being a parent is an immense responsibility, a 24/7 job that offers no sabbatical. It's a role I cherish. Kaitlyn, my toddler, and Emma, my baby, are totally dependent on Jason and me at this stage of their lives. It will get easier for us when they are older and can dress, bathe, and feed themselves. But until that point, it's a hands-on duty and we must communicate properly about concerns and issues along our journey.

Bottom line: You're in this together for the long haul – for better or worse. Despite the economic downturn, you can survive its impact and excel through effective communication.

Chapter 3

Finances: Are We On the Right Path?

These are trying financial times for countless working mothers in the US and their families. As of summer 2011, eight million former US workers are searching for jobs; an astounding six million have given up. Corporations have matched earnings reports from 2006, but with 2.5 million fewer workers. Most workers who lost their jobs during this recession have been unemployed for over six months – a majority over 12 months – and are fearful they will never recover economically. And the companies that show the most dramatic increases in profitability also add the fewest workers.

In January 2011, I read in the *Philadelphia Inquirer* about how the long-term jobless were losing hope and prospects. This resonated with me because Jason had been out of work for so long, and we both were discouraged about his full-time career prospects. The article featured Donna Oxford, a 53-year-old who was laid off from an e-commerce company in December 2007. Six months after she was laid off, she gained custody of her 2-year-old grandson to keep him out of foster care. She wrote a moving poem, 'Today I Lost a Tooth', that recalled her state of poverty, lack of medical and dental insurance, and so forth.

I read this in a local Starbucks with my two daughters and was moved to tears by her story. Millions of mothers – single and married – have found themselves in unfortunate situations today, concerned about how they will support their children. I knew that cold day in January I had to write this book to address these unprecedented obstacles women were facing.

Sally Andrews (name changed), a working mother who lives north of Boston, is one mother who has learned how to trim expenses. Married with an eight-month-old child, she recently left the big corporate job for a job at a small company closer to home. She wanted to spend more time playing with him rather than commuting back and forth from her corporate job. 'I took a good-size pay cut when I changed jobs so we've had to really watch our spending. I used to buy my lunch every day, but now I make it at home, which has increased my grocery bill some, but it's manageable,' she said.

Andrews also learned she doesn't need to keep up with 'the Jones.' 'Buying things from the Dollar Store or discounted places doesn't make me cheap or poor – I think of it as thrifty. I've taken in a lot of hand-me-downs for my son and have shopped at consignment shops. Babies outgrow things fairly quickly so some items don't need to be purchased brand new,' she admitted.' I found a great consignment shop in a well-to-do neighborhood that has brand name items for my son at a fraction of the original price. They've been gently worn but no one can tell unless I tell them.'

Andrews thinks you just have to know where to cut corners and where you cannot skimp: 'I will skimp on clothing and housewares (superficial things) but I won't skimp on food or healthcare (things that directly affect me and my family's health).'

Jason and I have held back on what now seem to us to be frivolous purchases such as clothing, dinners out, vacations and travel. We won't cut corners when it comes to our family's well-being. Quality food and healthcare are imperative.

Revised Spending Plans

How has the Great Recession affected other working mothers' financial decisions? Kimberly Foss, CFP, a personal finance expert in Roseville, California, said almost all of her clients, working or retired, have put into place a revised 'spending plan' which matched their incomes – either as W-2 wages or retirement income. On average, Foss has seen her clients cut usually 20 percent to 30 percent of their spending plan's expenses over the past 36 months.

'My mothers are much more cost conscious and are making purchases in bulk, placing what could be "wants" on a "watch list" for 30 days before purchasing the items,' Foss said. 'For example, perhaps a new suit for work would be placed on the watch list. After 30 days, they revisit the items and typically the mother forgoes the new items because she has spotted a suitable replacement at a consignment store.'

Deana Arnett, CFP, a senior planning consultant at Financial Planning Services in Northern Virginia, said the Great Recession has caused people to hold onto their money more tightly. 'Mothers tend to be less of a risk-taker than fathers, and the recession has intensified that tendency. Mothers are inclined to look at ways to juggle all of the household responsibilities – getting the kids to school, making dinner, paying the bills,' she said. 'The Great Recession has forced them to look at how they can do things more efficiently and trim the fat.'

These challenging economic times have changed the advice some finance experts offer. Foss has advocated even if you have $5 million in the bank, to cut your spending down – to 65 percent 'needs,' 20 percent 'wants,' and 15 percent 'savings,' for example.

Arnett has always been a 'no debt adviser,' but she is anti-debt more now than ever. Before this recession, she never talked to her clients about coupon clipping or managing household budgets. She learned that many people cannot handle their household budgets. 'Many of my clients have busy working and family lives and simply don't have time to set up a budget,' Arnett confided. 'Today, I spend a lot more time talking to clients about the basics. While recessions are hard times, they are a great time for people to reset, re-evaluate, and even correct financial mistakes they've made in the past.'

Today, Arnett advises clients more to have their houses paid off. She helps clients pay their houses off early, use existing mortgages to do so, and avoid any refinancing.

Single Mother Struggles

Carol Lavis, one of the three founders of New Hope Pregnancy Resource Center in Bergen County, New Jersey, has helped countless young, single mothers get back on their feet and settle in careers. Established in 1985, New Hope, Inc., is an outreach organization that provides help for single first-time mothers and their babies. It provides subsidies for housing, daycare, education, and counseling. New Hope Pregnancy Resource Center is now staffed by 33 volunteers.

Lavis is a dear family friend – I have known her since I was a baby and played with her son in the sandbox as a toddler. I am amazed at the work she does to help young moms get situated in careers and establish decent lives for themselves and their young children. She shared with me the issues with which her clients are currently struggling.

Sharon (name changed) is a woman who is living with her parents. Because she does not have to pay rent, she is not as financially challenged as some of the others. 'However, she may have to take out loans for her education and for her car insurance. Living in Bergen County without a car is challenging to our mothers unless they live in an urban area where bus service is decent,' Lavis told me. 'Several of our clients live in towns with spotty bus service, so they are faced with needing a car and car insurance. There's a program called Dollar a Day Car Insurance that only amounts to $365 a year. Unfortunately it is only for certain clients, and it only covers liability so if a client is in a car accident and her car is totaled, end of story.'

Lavis also has Anna (name changed) in her program, a young woman who is attending Bergen Community College and is also working there. Anna is getting paid $900 a month, which is a windfall because she is also living at home.

Sometimes the young mothers have been forced out by their

parents. The stigma of 'unwed motherhood' remains strong in many areas; in other cases the 'grandparents' do not like the idea of having a baby in their home. In other cases, young mothers have become homeless via eviction or lack of a job or any funds; they may end up in a shelter temporarily.

'Some of them may really like it there; they may stay in the shelter for the maximum time which is typically a year, either pregnant or with their baby or toddler,' Lavis said. 'Others really hate the shelters – they plead with us to put them in an apartment. If they are 20 years old, we often go along with that, but we really don't like putting a 19-year-old in an apartment by herself.'

In contrast, Lavis often finds that once the baby is born, the grandparents fall head-over-heels in love with this new life and are more amenable to making room in their homes – and in their hearts – for the infant (and, by extension, the mother, their daughter).

Whenever New Hope is confident that two women are compatible, Lavis can get a two-bedroom, possibly a three-bedroom apartment for them – the babies can go in one room, and the women can sleep in another room or one can sleep on a couch. 'We can get a three-bedroom apartment for about $1,500 where each young mom is only responsible for $750 a month. We, and perhaps some other organizations, will help subsidize this,' she said. 'We have to be careful to abide by all the regulations of the Division of Youth and Family Services.'

County and state programs will also help moms get into apartments or other living situations. Lavis said that sometimes moms may get generous rental assistance. She has two moms in the program who each have a set of twins – they get generous subsidies from the county.

The current economic downturn is affecting these young working mothers negatively. Many of them are having trouble finding quality work that pays adequately and that will allow them to spend time with their babies.

'I have one whom I put in counseling because she told me the other day that she is having trouble getting out of bed in the morning. There are just too many things going on in her life that are negative,' Lavis said. 'We teach them to count the blessings they have. The father of her toddler is now in jail for 12 years; she doesn't want her young son to be visiting him. If someone in the family is incarcerated, the emotional stability of those in the relationship is more fragile. Bringing a young child to a jail obviously can be an issue.'

New Hope always stresses that the fathers need visitation time, but this can be done in a park or restaurant. The non-profit doesn't allow the fathers to come into any of the apartments it is subsidizing.

Part-time jobs with no benefits are a challenge for these mothers – New Hope pushes for them to go to college. 'We stress that once they are out in the workforce with a college degree, they are going to be making $10,000 to $15,000 more per year. That is going to make a big difference in their standard of living. This will enable them to get out of areas that are drug and crime infested,' Lavis said.

'We work with most of our mothers for three years. We have one delightful woman who only finished a year of high school. So our priority is to get her to get that GED. Once she gets that, we'll work on vocational examinations with her to find out what field she is drawn towards. We have a lot of women going into the medical field. In the past, we stayed with women for years; one became a doctor, another a dentist. J. became an osteopath in June 2011. She owes about $90,000 in loans, but she plans to have that paid back in nine years.'

A Second Income Is Paramount

I spoke with many mothers who think it is crucial for both spouses in the family to be working. Anna M. Aquino is a writer and a stay-at-home mom in this situation. This year her youngest started kindergarten and while her writing career is beginning to take off, they're still in need of a second income. 'This has presented a predicament – looking for a job that will meet our needs and time constraints so I can still be there for the kids and make a second income. I'm looking for a part-time job; I also have a book coming out this March,' she said with pride.

Aquino is particular about what she's looking for in a job given the hours she's available. 'I always considered myself a working mother even though I stayed at home. While I haven't made a lot as a writer yet, I never considered myself not working,' she said. 'We've been okay over these years, but the second income would definitely be nice. It's a challenge explaining what I've been doing the last ten years. I worked a few times part-time throughout the years, but nothing consistent.'

The economic downturn has affected the cost of Aquino's home. Since they bought it, their house has probably lost $70,000 if the 30 percent decline holds true. 'Central Florida has been home to one of the biggest real estate market bubble bursts. It gained probably $60–$70,000 after we bought it, and then the bubble broke,' Aquino admitted. 'It's dropped that much in the last few years. If we were looking to sell that might be enough to freak us out. But we're not looking to sell at the moment, and so I refuse to worry about it.'

Aquino said it has been hard for her family to live on one income, and that has affected their stress level. 'But every time we look at our alternatives, we know we've made the right choice. Daycare and aftercare are really expensive. When you look at the math, I would be working full-time to pay someone else to raise our kids and would only be bringing in a few hundred dollars a month,' she said. 'It just didn't seem worth it to us. I realized that I had been given a gift to stay at home. As much as I had struggled with that choice, I have no regrets.'

Lora Sasiela, MSW, financial therapist and founder of FinanciallySmitten.com, sees scarcity of time as the biggest financial hurdle for working mothers. 'Between meal planning, grocery shopping, laundry, and soccer-practice car-pooling, it's very easy for money management to take a back seat. To work with the reality of a mom's time constraints, I always suggest streamlining and automating financial management as much as possible,' Sasiela said. 'Thankfully, we have ever-evolving technology to assist with this.'

For example, Sasiela encourages leveraging online banking to its fullest. 'You can set up monthly payments and auto deposits into linked checking accounts. Aggregate sites such as www.mint.com make money management a breeze, pulling in all your transactions across various financial institutions (credit cards, mortgage, bank accounts, student loans, and so forth) into one centralized spot,' she said. 'And as we move more into the smart phone app world, there are more options to manage one's money literally "on the go."'

Anxiety over Job Security

The recent economic climate has created a lot of anxiety for people – around job security, in particular. Sasiela said one thing that has become more valuable is the comfort of an emergency fund cushion. If someone does not have one set up, then this is one of the first things she suggests to remedy this anxiety. 'Whereas in the past the typical advice was to have three to six months of living expenses saved, that benchmark is no longer optimal. People need to factor in the reality of how long they expect it would take to get another job in their particular industry, what other resources they may have to generate income, and most importantly, what savings amount actually provides them a sense of comfort,' Sasiela said.

Financial consciousness and clarity are always in style, no matter what the current economic conditions, and good financial management is timeless. Sasiela's financial therapy clients find the clearer and more conscious they become about money and financial decision-making, the less anxiety they have. Something is empowering and calming, knowing you are on top of your financial life.

The tried and true 'buy low, sell high' wisdom often gets tossed out the window when people watch the news and witness the stock market doing its roller-coaster thing. 'This is a critical point where people can make very deleterious financial decisions and actually lose money because they are not abiding by the "buy and hold" method that will reap returns in the long run,' Sasiela said. 'If a client is experiencing a lot of anxiety due to the market's volatility, I often suggest going on a media diet for a week and integrating some stress reduction techniques. They are often surprised by how much better they feel!'

A current issue I face as a small business owner is adequate payment for my services. I have had to turn down work because it did not meet monetary expectations. With over ten years of writing and publicity experience as a self-employed professional, I won't work for less than what I am worth. As they say, time is money – I want to make sure I am spending my work time wisely. I do love being in business for myself but it has its challenges.

Through my book research, I connected with impressive self-employed mothers who faced financial struggles, but surpassed them to establish successful businesses. I loved hearing these stories!

At age 31, Nancy D. Butler, with Above All Else, faced grave financial challenges. While in the process of a divorce, she took her two daughters and, with no child support, alimony, or other source of income, moved 70 miles away and started her own business.

At the new location, Butler was offered a salaried position at a higher pay than she ever had before, but realized they were hiring her at 'the top of the ladder,' leaving her no place to grow. She did not want a job. She needed a career.

'I knew nothing about saving, investing, or financial planning and had never owned a CD, mutual fund, or anything other than a savings account. I told myself that even if the business didn't work out, the knowledge and experience I would gain would be worth it since what I would learn about managing money would help me to raise my children,' Butler told me.

Butler built the business from scratch into one of the top asset management and financial planning practices in the country. She earned the certified financial planner (CFP) designation and acquired extensive training in financial planning and asset management. With approximately $200 million in assets under management and 1,200 clients, after 25 years in business, she sold her practice.

Butler is now a national speaker helping individuals live a successful life and realize their dreams, and helping business owners do a better job for their clients and improve their bottom line.

Overcoming Financial Issues

Andrea Pokorny, founder of www.MainstreamMom.com, gave up her corporate career three years ago to be home with her three kids and had financial obstacles in her way after she left. 'I could no longer take leaving them with practically strangers for nine plus hours every day. I had been battling with the decision ever since I was on maternity leave with my first little girl,' Pokorny said. 'But when my dad died suddenly, things were put into perspective rather abruptly, which caused me to think in a whole new way.'

Once Pokorny left her career, she tried several new ventures to make money from home, attempting to replace the missed income (she was bringing home over $70,000 per year, and now this was gone). She fell short time and again, but not without succeeding in building a pile of debt. 'We had a mortgage, normal expenses like every household, credit card debt (skyrocketing), and I was seven months pregnant with our third child when my husband got an *email* from his employer telling him he just got a drastic pay-cut,' Pokorny confided. 'In a very short time frame, our income went from well over $100,000 down to $25,000. We were in a bit over our heads!'

Add the healthcare for their new little baby boy (who was helicoptered to a neo-natal intensive care unit shortly after birth), Pokorny's mom suddenly passing away, plus her futile attempts to build a home-based business and racking up debt. Their lives and finances were deteriorating rapidly.

Pokorny admitted she was horrible with money and had been her entire life. 'I never budgeted, always lived paycheck to paycheck, and I never cared to learn the important basics of managing money. Obviously this was our wake-up call,' she said. 'Thankfully my husband was offered a better job within only one week. We had to relocate and sell our home. We began renting and rebuilding our lives, knowing exactly what our goal was – to live debt free.'

Fast forward to today. Pokorny created a sizable income working from her home computer. They've made strides in becoming debt free (almost totally there). The way in which she got through it? 100 percent self-education. 'I became a library-going, website-searching, reading fanatic, and basically got my act together. During my struggles, I created my website to help other mothers looking for financial security,' said Pokorny. 'I am now also a marketing manager for another site online.'

So despite many bumps in the road once she left her career, Pokorny has been able to create another income working from her home office.

Stacy Francis, founder of Savvy Ladies, a non-profit organization dedicated to empowering women to take control of their finances and achieve a richer life, said something interesting happened in her latest Savvy Ladies telephone conference. When one woman told the group that her husband's sloppy attitude toward money was so frustrating to her and that she wanted to divorce him for this reason alone, every woman in the group expressed their support. 'Several of the married women even told her they could relate because they were having similar issues in their marriages,' Francis said.

Indeed, one of the most common reasons couples split is financial disagreement. Here's how you can overcome financial hurdles and set a plan for the future with your spouse or partner:

- *Create a budget.* 'Sit down together, and put your expenses and financial goals on paper. Be realistic, and make sure that sticking to the budget won't require too much effort,' said Francis. 'Remember that budgets are like diets – they never work if they're unrealistic.'

  New York City-based Jeanne Brutman, a fee-based financial planner for business owners and individuals, agrees. 'Consider the usual: housing, electricity, garbage, water, landline phone, cable, internet, cellular phone, childcare or support, food (grocery, eating at work, ordering in), transportation (car payments, gas, tolls, parking or bus, subway, transit, cab), insurance outside of deductions from paycheck (renters, home, umbrella, car, health, dental/vision, life, disability, Medicare, long-term care, and so forth), debt (car, student loans, credit cards, personal), drug store, prescriptions, pet supplies, home or car maintenance, clothing, dry cleaning, laundry, and lastly charity, entertainment, and so forth,' she said. 'Please account for 5 or 10 percent if possible to go towards savings. Do not spend more than 20 percent of what you make on debt. If you only focus on paying off debt, you get what you focus on!'

- *Hire a professional.* The financial experts I spoke to agreed on this. 'Find a certified financial planner in your area, interview them and pick one that understands where you are in your financial journey,' said Arnett. 'Seek out a financial planner who will sit down and prioritize your goals, put money figures next to them, and then show you how to reach those objectives.'

'A person only has 168 hours a week. 60 to 80 (say 70) are for work, 14 are for eating, 49 are for sleeping, 7 are for personal hygiene, 17 are for housekeeping and food shopping... that leaves 11 hours for other stuff,' said Brutman. 'I spend 70 hours a week on my profession and have done that for 10 years. That's 36,400 hours on financial planning. Get help – we just have more time to get you to the information you need faster.' Sasiela often suggests her financial therapy clients work with a financial planner to get clear on their future goals and how best to manage their resources to meet them.

- *Communicate and work together.* 'It seems so basic, but you have to agree that there is a hurdle, what that hurdle is, and then commit to a strategy to get past it. It takes a conscious effort to get past a hurdle, whether it's financial, emotional, or something else,' said Arnett. 'When you agree up front on the hurdle itself and the tactic for overcoming it, then you get strength in numbers. You're not facing it alone, and that means something.'

  Many couples fail to discuss their financial differences. 'Approach them in a calm, non-threatening way, and focus on finding constructive solutions that both of you agree will work,' said Francis. 'Whether you intend it or not, the way you manage your money will affect your spouse as well. Make sure he or she is comfortable with your spending and investment habits.'
- *Keep a credit card for emergencies only.* 'As you may have noticed, when you don't use a card, the issuing bank tends

to up your limit to tempt you to use it. You can, but only when you have no other choice,' advised Francis. 'Remove from your wallet: all credit cards but one for emergency (defined as life-threatening need such as needing to get towed because of a car accident); and all cash except for $40 that you only use when you cannot use a debit card,' Brutman advised. 'For all spending, use a debit card linked to your monthly account.'

- *Determine what is of most importance.* Separate the 'wants' from the 'needs.' For example, Foss said a need may be funding tuition for your child's future, while buying the latest trendy clothes from Abercrombie is a 'want.' Teach your children by example, she said – by sacrificing a 'want' today for a 'need' of a college education years down the road.

Determining what is truly of importance is tough because what may seem important to one person can sound like a discretionary item to another. Take for instance, private school. 'For many families, it is a priority for their children to attend private school. However, there are public schools children can be sent to for free, not to mention, your tax money already goes there,' Arnett said. 'The reality is that during hard times, sometimes gratification has to be delayed.'

Foss advocates you and your spouse create a 'top ten' money goal list on your own and then compare the lists with one another. 'Create a common goal list from the two separate ones. Typically, financial goals are much different from each spouse's perspective,' she said. 'Create a common list – create a sense of financial partnership to work towards your combined list.'

For example, on Foss' top ten list, she chose to accelerate their mortgage payment to pay off the house in five years rather than 15. Her husband's goal was to fund his children's (her stepchildren's) college education funds. They ended up choosing to downsize their home to reduce the mortgage and create more cash flow, thereby accomplishing both goals.

I learned many valuable lessons from the financial experts I interviewed. When you are discussing finances with your spouse, a key question you should address is, 'How many kids do we want to have?' Are you both in agreement on this?

I know some women who have had surprise pregnancies and are now on their second and third children; these babies had not been part of their plans, but they accepted the pregnancies with open hearts and minds.

Be realistic: How many children can you afford? It's a different generation from that of our parents and grandparents when it was common to have large families. Now, college tuition costs have skyrocketed. Daycare expenses are also a factor to consider – multiple toddlers in quality care can be a second mortgage payment.

I'm 40 now and can say with certainty we won't be having any more kids. That's based on financial – and health – considerations.

Chapter 4

Romance: Is It Still Possible?

Working mothers are under more pressure today than ever before – due to high unemployment, fear of losing one's job, longer work hours, reduced salaries, and so forth. For many career moms like me, romance is often at the bottom of our priority list. We have work deadlines, toddler schedules to manage, and meals to shop for and prepare. Putting romance on that list makes it feel like one more chore.

An issue I struggle with – along with countless other career moms – is fatigue at the day's end. I will often go to sleep earlier than Jason, not long after I put Kaitlyn to bed and do some work at my computer. Couples do not spend a lot of alone time together as a couple. And when we do carve out such time, we spend a portion of it making sure that all the other chores and commitments are covered.

How is the intimacy level in your marriage or partnership? Do you spend more time apart than together? Do you wonder how you can recapture the loving feelings and connection that brought the two of you together? If so, then it is time to re-evaluate priorities and see where you can fit in some quality alone time for you and your significant other – without screaming kids in the picture.

Let's agree on some basics. On the one hand, every marriage could be improved in some aspect; no marriage is perfect. Google returns over six million results for 'improving my relationship.' On the other hand, many couples often postpone any attentiveness to each other once the babies arrive. Frankly, it is easier for them to place attention on their children ahead of their spouse's – and their own – intimacy needs.

The biggest complaint men have about their wives or significant other once they have the baby is not women's post-baby weight nor the baby keeping them up all night, said Dr. Leslie Seppinni, PsyD, LMFT, and author of *Who Is Casey Anthony? Understanding the Motherly Motivation to Murder* (Dunham Books, 2012). 'Rather, men's biggest complaint is that they feel left out and they miss you. Many men are not emotionally prepared for your attention to be split 85 to 99 percent to the baby and 1 to 15 percent to them,' she said. 'They don't feel they are getting the same amount of your time, attention and affection.'

Especially if you treated them as the center of your world pre-'baby makes three.' 'You have to try as best as you can to remember that although you may be exhausted and overwhelmed, he still needs to know you need him and miss him as well. It's tough to take your attention away from the baby but necessary to have a healthy relationship with your man and the father of your child,' said Seppinni.

Within the first six months you must remind yourself of who you are. 'I'm not asking you to cater to your man by dressing up, putting make-up on daily and all the other expectations that go with being a woman but do make an effort to take off the sweats, comb your hair and throw on some lip gloss and blush one to two days a week to remind him you're still in there,' she said.

Seppinni said you have layers of relationships and you have to respect and nurture those relationships. The first relationship you have is with yourself, the second is with your husband; the third ring is you, your husband and kids; the last ring is your individual relationship and time with each child.

Working mothers have a hard enough time trying to split their energy between their work and their children. 'Throw housework, exercise, time with friends, and time with their partners into the mix, and there simply are not enough hours in the day! Some of the biggest obstacles to romance are: fatigue, low desire, no time, and body concerns,' said Julie Jeske, a sex and relationship counselor in Portland, Oregon. 'If your partner isn't being supportive or helping out with your child(ren), you might add resentment to the list. There are so many things on working moms' to-do lists, sex and romance can sometimes get lost in the shuffle.'

Less Time Together

Esure.com offers some remarkable statistics about couples and their time together:

- Couples currently spend less than an hour a day talking in person. Almost one in five (18 percent) spend only 15 minutes speaking face to face.
- The typical couple now spends just 3 hours and 40 minutes together daily. This includes 51 minutes watching TV in silence and 37 minutes on household chores.
- Of the couples polled, 27 percent admitted that they do not get the chance to relax and have a decent conversation until the weekend.
- And 22 percent enjoy dinner together just three evenings per week or less.
- Even while together, 41 percent of couples send texts, emails, or use social networking sites such as Facebook.com to relay messages rather than speak to one another.
- The average couple sends an overwhelming 1,002 texts and almost 400 emails to each other every year.
- A further 13 percent of those polled admitted checking Facebook.com to keep track of what their other half is up to.

Keep Couple Commitment Distinct from Family Relationships

Dr. Jill Kristal, a psychologist from the New York area, often hears new parents and parents of young children say they don't go out or they don't go out without their children. She agrees couples need adult time away from their kids, even for a few hours a week. The sooner you begin this practice, the easier it is to keep it going. 'My own mother came to stay and insisted that my husband and I go out for dinner alone, just days after our first child was born. As hesitant as we were, it set the stage for "date night" that continued throughout our children's lives,' she said.

So the marriage needs to be held distinct from the family relationship. 'Taking time to be alone together, doing some of the things you did together pre-baby, making time to focus on each other and remembering that without the two of you, the baby wouldn't be there, should help keep the priorities straight and romance intact,' she added.

Remember – you were with your partner before you had a baby. 'Your partner is your primary relationship. When you add a baby into the mix, your mate might feel left out. One day your baby will become an adult and move on into his or her own life,' said Jeske. 'Your spouse will still be with you then. How can you focus on your relationship now so that you want to spend time together 18 years from now? Remember what drew you to your partner. Remember the fun and loving things you used to (and hopefully still) do. Don't forget that loving bond you share.'

Keeping Date Night

I strongly believe it is important to set alone time for you and your spouse as often as possible. If your parents or in-laws live nearby, then ask them to watch the children Saturday nights so you can go out to dinner and a movie. If you have a neighbor with young kids, then ask them to babysit one night at your house. Return the favor and watch their kids another night.

If you don't get out enough, tell your partner that you would like to go out more together as a couple. Jason and I don't go out nearly as often as we should. It's an issue I brought up to him and hope will be addressed. He would rather stay in, cook, and watch movies or games on television. I get frustrated with staying home every weekend. I have mom friends I go out with some nights, but miss nights out with Jason – which we had pre-kids.

'If there is an opportunity for the two of you to have a date night, then take it. Don't bring the baby with you,' agreed Seppinni. 'You have to be willing to let go.' When asked about dating on a limited budget, Seppinni said there are many things you can do – hiking, picnics, movies. There are sites like Groupon where you can get 50 percent off dinners at great restaurants. You don't have to leave the house – you can have a picnic in your own living room and play a romantic game.

Trish's Struggles over Time

Trish Adkins, a mommy blogger from Philadelphia, shared her current romantic struggles with her spouse Mike; they have been a couple since her junior year of high school. 'I was always the ambitious career girl – and my husband always moved for me. Our Vermont move was for a job; as was our move back to the Philly region. For a chunk of my career, I made more than him, had longer hours, traveled more, and had mass amounts of responsibility,' Adkins confided. 'Mike is an engineer, and he has had ambition – and he is amazing at his job. But I was always so ridiculously public about my goals and really, I had an enormous ego. Then my first child was born really early, and my priorities shifted.'

Adkins' first child Lily was diagnosed with a brain tumor. She began not to care about work. Mike, in contrast, began to work harder to support their family. 'This continued through Lily's treatment and recovery; we both worked through it all – we had to (or risk financial disaster). The difference: I shifted my ambition to motherhood. My husband worked with both career and parenthood ambition,' she continued. 'Our second child was also born early and during my maternity leave, I withdrew from my full-time consulting position. I was so happy to be able to focus on motherhood, fully.'

These events have slowly made their relationship shift. Mike thought he was getting a career girl – and often remarked that he would be happy to be a stay-at-home dad. 'While my internal ambition-shift has been gradual for me – for Mike I think it feels sudden and like a slap in the face. He often remarks that I was supposed to be the one with the big job. I know he believes raising our children is the most important job – but at the same time, he struggles with me taking time to freelance write (for a pittance compared to the money I made before as a PR profes-sional) and teach yoga (which is basically for gas money and sometimes actually costs money),' she confided. 'Now I want to just be with my kids, write and teach. So what if our house needs to be painted or there are just a couple bucks left in the bank – we can always make more money.'

Like many couples, arguments about money and finances are their biggest – and most romance-killing – issue. Adkins works about 20 hours away from her family a week. 'My husband doesn't see it fully – or understand it. And so much of this is because I don't communicate the time and the return to him in an effective way,' she said. 'Time also kills the romance – we have so little time together – especially alone, outside the home during normal hours. Babysitters cost money. Date nights cost time that could be used to work on the house or clean or write or something. I think we often put ourselves last.'

'It's the Economy, Silly'

The economy has added more stress. 'With one of us working full-time – and essentially having the stable income – the uncertain economic state is frightening. It's not something we talk about a lot, but it's sitting there like an elephant in the room,' she concluded.

For countless women, the current economy is adding stress to their marriage and the romantic elements of the marriage. Many working mothers with whom I spoke are silently focused on this situation. A lower household income equates with less money for date nights as well as family fun time, such as vacations, entertainment, and dinners.

The unemployed and the self-employed (like me) face even greater pressures than the specter of income impact somewhere down the road. Finding suitable job openings or winning new clients when business is slower – these are immediate strains. At the end of a long day, when these financial pressures – and mounting unpaid bills – are on your mind (as well as the usual juggling of kids' needs and work schedules), romance hits the back burner.

The number one challenge for women who have babies and are working is absolute exhaustion, Seppinni said. The second challenge is getting men to understand why they're exhausted. 'Up until the economic downturn, a lot of men irrespective of demographics and socio-economics still refused, denied or simply didn't realize how hard it is to be a SAHM. Until circumstances forced them to make the change to becoming a SAHD (at least for the time being),' Seppinni said.

More men are respecting how truly demanding it can be. 'They are also realizing that although there is a valuable intrinsic reward in being a housewife, it can also feel lonely and thankless at times, especially when they are trying to take care of the endless list of: get the kids ready for school, clean the house, get the kids to do their chores, help with homework, doctors' appointments, make dinner, carpool, shop for groceries, etc.,' said Seppinni. 'On top of also now taking care of some of their working wives' needs as she once did to emotionally support him, they are scratching their heads realizing, "This isn't as easy as I thought it was."'

Seppinni predicted we'll see over generations to follow more women openly and truthfully speaking their minds as to their personal feelings about being a mom, regardless if they are stay-at-home or working mothers. This is the first generation of women in their late thirties through to fifties who are sharing information, she said. As a result of supportive websites for women, social media and blogs, women are willing to be interviewed about how hard it is to be a mother and be human without the harsh judgment of themselves and other mothers (women).

Communicate Your Stress

If jobs are less secure and money is tighter because of the current economy, then lives will become more stressful. Kristal said the key here is communication. 'Human beings find it terribly difficult to be vulnerable, and share their fears and worries. It is easier to blame, distance, and distort, but these approaches to stress and problems only compound existing tensions. Couples who weather the storms of stress in their marriage are couples who can talk to one another, learn to "fight" well, and problem solve,' she admitted. 'They get to the heart of the issue in a way that expresses the difficulty as a problem that needs a solution, as opposed to something wrong with one or the other person. From this comes brainstorming and trying out of different solutions until the problem is resolved or compromise is reached.'

Kristal's advice is clear:

- Acknowledge that the route to successful resolutions 'can be lengthy and circuitous.'
- At various times, one or the other partner will need to take the lead.
- Keeping the relationship as the priority 'can help get derailed conversations back on track.'
- Focusing on what is really important can reduce stress by pushing some of the stressors to the margins.

Focus on the Marriage Trunk of the Family Tree

How do you keep a romance alive once baby makes three? Kristal said the question provides clues to the answer, namely, *romance* and *alive*. 'It is important to remember that a marriage is a living thing, and, like any plant, requires ongoing nourishment and attention to thrive and grow. In comments I have heard many times, couples believe that they can and should put their children first, and themselves and their marriage in the dusty corners of the garden shed,' Kristal said. 'The truth is that marriage is hard work, and, along with raising children, it is likely to be the most difficult task you will ever undertake.'

It is up to you and your partner to make your relationship work. Kristal said the metaphor of the family tree is apt here as it depicts a strong trunk, the foundation of all that emerges from it. 'Marriage and the couple's relationship should form the foundation of the tree and family life. So, couples need to shift the perspective on their relationship and invest as much time, energy and creativity in each other as they do their children and other commitments. We often use romance to woo our partners and drop it once the relationship is secure,' she admitted. 'We need to realign this way of thinking. People like novelty and excitement; we like being thought of on occasions other than our birthdays and gift-card holidays. We like being acknowledged and appreciated for things big and small. More than sex, these are the reasons primarily given for having an affair.'

Amy Klein's Story

Amy Klein (name changed), a mom blogger and mother of two (eight months and 2 years old), said their recent relationship issues are that she and her husband Sam (name changed) don't appreciate the other person's role. 'I'm jealous of the fact that he gets to go to lunch with friends, have the use of my two hands for assistance on his home jobs, and access the bathroom when he wants. He's jealous of the fact that I don't have the pressure of being the primary breadwinner that has to fund putting our kids through college,' she said.

At times, they both seem to want acknowledgments for the work they do. 'We focus on the little stuff that the other gets to do instead of the big picture and sacrifices the other is making for our family. Yes, the economy plays a role in the stress on our relationship,' Klein said. 'Sam is an investment banker so we are greatly affected by the economy and have had to start over a bit. At the end of the day, we are spent after we finally get the kids to bed, and we both jump on our computers until bedtime.'

Klein doesn't feel any romance. In addition to blogging, she is exhausted from the pressure of keeping the kids and house running. 'We get very little time to do the things we used to love – all our energy is put into the kids and family activities (which I love),' she admitted. 'Sam and I are working on finding a way to connect again. We are different people now – still in love. Still best friends, but different people.'

When Klein is completely stressed, she thinks there will be a time when she and Sam will 'have a ton of free time to travel the world again and just hang out and do nothing.' She realizes there will also be a time when her boys will not need her like they do now. 'I won't be their best pal, their world, their number one... so I hug and kiss them while I can. I stay up all night with them and I take on the adventures every day,' she said.

Intimacy and Affection Levels

Klein's situation has affected their intimacy level. 'When I put the boys to bed it is a ticking clock as to when they will wake up... especially the eight-month-old. My head is just not focused on sex,' she confided. 'I actually feel really bad for my husband. He is a really good sport about it, but it does cause a lot of tension.'

Kristal has spoken to multitudes of women like Klein who stop buying and wearing sexy lingerie, who balk at negligees and sex toys presented by their husbands, who scoff at romantic weekends and the need for small intimacies. She believes all these things are important in an ongoing way and for the long haul. 'Individually as women, we ought to continue to find ways to feel pretty, sexy, and romantic, as much for ourselves as for our partners. Regardless of expanding waistlines, wrinkles, and gray hair, feeling inwardly attractive and good about ourselves will help us want to share ourselves with our partner,' she said.

Ideas about what is romantic can vary widely between individuals and couples. We need to communicate to let our partners know what we like, want, and need. 'People aren't mind readers, and people's likes and needs change over time. So let your partner know clearly what you like and what you don't, what makes you feel romantic and what doesn't. However, you also want to be willing to try new things,' Kristal concluded. 'Novelty brings excitement, and can add humor and fun to your relationship. Finally, romantic gestures don't need to be big; they just need to happen. Being greeted at the door with a kiss, slipping a note in a suitcase or PDA – these are all romantic gestures that don't require lots of planning or expense, but they let you love and be loved and that is the greatest romance of all.'

At least 62 percent of working parents are too stressed out to have sex with their spouses, according to a national survey commissioned by Care.com Inc. They are also too frazzled to go to the gym or keep in contact with their friends.

According to the same survey, 25 percent of working parents say they would have more flexibility in their lives if they left their current jobs for jobs that pay less – even considerably less. Why would they do this? Because more flexibility might improve their sex lives.

The company's survey, conducted online with responses from 600 parents in February–March 2011, offers a small window to parents' stressed-out souls. A press release reports 35 percent of parents cite work as the most stressful element in their lives, while 24 percent say finding a trusted nanny or babysitter is more stressful than keeping a spouse happy or excelling at work.

'While the White House recently announced the great strides of women in the workplace, this survey shows that the work-life balance for so many working parents remains elusive,' Wendy Sachs, editor of Care.com, said. 'It's no surprise that moms who are toting buzzing BlackBerries in their bags, chock-full of work emails, can feel tapped out and not eager for sex.'

What are ways time-pressed working mothers can turn around this trend and improve their sex lives? Two sex experts weigh in:

- Know your body, know what feels good and know what you crave. 'One of the easiest ways to keep the romance alive is to focus on things you really like and find pleasurable. If you plan date nights that are exciting, you can make sure you are doing something you enjoy,' Jeske said. 'If you know that you are going to have the kind of sex you enjoy, you are more likely to look forward to it!'

- Know what you like, initiate it or ask for it. 'Your partner wants to please you and he might not have as many obstacles as you do right now (especially the hormones and body changes). Tell him what would make you more interested in sex or physical intimacy,' said Jeske. 'If you know you need more sleep in order to be present, let your partner know so you can find a solution. If you need more romance or verbal affirmations, it's okay to ask for that too.'

- Manage your expectations. Sex after baby may feel different. 'If you get too caught up in expectations you might feel like a failure. Be open to what sex feels like now. If it's disappointing you can shift it,' said Jeske. 'Don't worry about what other people are doing, or how often they are having sex. Focus on your relationship and what you want it to look like.'

- To make sure romance stays alive, schedule it. When Jeske talks to couples about scheduling dates or sex, they are often resistant. Their biggest complaint is that it takes all of the spontaneity out of it. 'Just because you schedule something doesn't mean that it can't be fun or sponta-neous. If you can look at the idea of scheduling differently, it will help. Think about all of the things you do in your life. How many are scheduled? Work, working out, doctor's appointments – often if these things aren't on our calendar, they won't happen. Why not have a special day for sex?'

- Jeske has an interesting point: if you think back to an earlier time of your relationship, you probably scheduled dates and sex without even realizing in. 'When couples are courting and plan to get together on Friday night, that is scheduling a date. And if those couples are sexually active, they are probably expecting to have sex that night. In the earlier days of your relationship you probably looked forward to your dates and those times you could be sexual,' she concluded. 'You may have fantasized about them, bought a special outfit, shaved your legs and looked forward to them. Can't your current date nights be the same? If you know you are having a romantic date on Friday... then you have all week to think about it and get excited. You can send each other anticipatory texts or talk about looking forward to it as the week goes on.'

You pencil everything else into your planner. If you can schedule doctor's appointments, hair appointments, and so forth, why not set a few hours aside for each other?

Bringing Intimacy Back

Andrea Lyons, CEO/founder of Bring Back Desire, LLC, agrees

intimacy with our husband or partner is key. 'Challenges to a working mom are always about how to be present for everyone, including herself,' she said. 'We often cruise through the day like Road Runner – six inches off the ground! Mix in serious life challenges, and no way are we in our bodies.'

Lyons has been with her DH (darling husband) for 26 years, 23 of them married. During these years they have earned two MBAs; had a live delivery at five months (Marcy), a stillborn at seven months (Jack), and a miscarriage at three months; two successful outcomes – Hunter and Matt; lost one huge business and one semi-huge business; moved seven times, five of which were within five years – across country – and with children; faced health challenges and bankruptcy, among other trials.

How can you keep the fires going during life's traumatic events? 'You create the space and time for sensuality and intimacy,' said Lyons. 'As a woman, I needed to figure out what that looked and felt like for me, and put it into place.'

Lyons' journey started when she was trying to conceive after the age of 35. 'It became all about the ovulation schedule. There was no way I was going to conceive a precious treasure without having an orgasm, so I sent DH down to the local erotica store and had him bring back some racy erotica books – written by women for women,' she admitted. 'I'd light candles, play music, throw a sexy outfit on – but it took the erotica reading to get me out of my head. Just like the experts say, 20 to 30 minutes of this type of reading brought immediate arousal – which was a good thing because I was usually "performing" between meetings!'

Fast forward to having two toddlers – who hold and pull and cling to your body all day. 'My DH would look at me, and I'd cringe – don't touch me! Again, I found a way to create romance for us. Drop the precious treasures at a friend's house, use my mood-enhancing techniques to set the tone, add food and beverage, and massage oil... without kids at home, "swinging from the chandeliers" was a possibility,' Lyons said.

During a big company startup, growth, and then rampdown – a full-time nanny saved their lives. 'When the dot com turned into a dot bomb, marriage counseling saved our lives. Communication during scary times can become very negative, with a lot of finger pointing. Counseling can help shift the messaging to each other,' she continued.

Most important: it was allowing Lyons to receive love, attention, affection, and sensual pleasure from DH. 'When we lit our candles, we agreed to leave the "crap" outside the door and remember why we fell in love with each other and why we each were so special. Then we got down to creating some serious arousal,' she said.

Men's brains are wired to provide and protect – that's why physical intimacy is so important to them. Lyons said they want to provide their woman with a fabulous sensual experience. When a group of 2,000 men were surveyed on the question 'What do you want from a woman in bed?' the number one answer was: A turned-on woman who wants to be there.

Lyons uses the tagline 'everything a gal needs to get out of her head and get back into bed' because women hang out in their to-do lists or their Worry Lists. 'It takes effort, strategy, and execution to get the lust going, but heck, women are terrific at this! Regular orgasms help lower cortisol (reduce stress), increase estrogen, balance the thyroid, and they get us grounded into our bodies,' she concluded.

Part 2

Health Issues

Chapter 5

Sleep Deprivation: How Can I Cope with It?

Many career moms today with babies or toddlers don't get enough sleep, a reality few moms would dispute. Such lack of sleep may affect their mental clarity and physical health. Returning to work after maternity leaves that are often too brief, many mothers struggle with feeding their infants during the night and functioning on the job during the day. Infant feeding responsibilities largely fall on the mothers' shoulders, even when other chores are shared.

Working mothers are two and a half times more likely than working fathers to have their sleep interrupted to take care of others, according to the finding of a University of Michigan study released in December 2010. This provides the first known nationally representative data documenting substantial gender differences in getting up at night, mainly with babies and small children. Women's sleep interruptions last longer – an average of 44 minutes for women, compared to about 30 minutes for men.

'Interrupted sleep is a burden borne disproportionately by women,' said sociologist Sarah Burgard, a researcher at the U-M Institute for Social Research (ISR). 'And this burden may not only affect the health and well-being of women but also contribute to continuing gender inequality in earnings and career advancement.'

For the study, Burgard analyzed time-diary data from approximately 20,000 working parents from 2003 to 2007, drawn from the US Census Bureau's American Time Use Survey. She found the gender gap in sleep interruptions was greatest during women's prime childbearing and child-rearing years of the twenties and thirties. Among dual-career couples with a child under the age of 1, 32 percent of women reported sleep interruptions to take care of the baby, compared with just 11 percent of men. (The study was funded by the National Institute of Child Health and Human Development, the National Institute on Aging, and the Sloan Foundation.)

Sleep Issues

For each of my daughters, I breastfed them and would awaken during the night when they were hungry. The toughest phase was the first few months, when they required the most attention. It got easier when they were able to sleep five or six hours at a time. I found this early stage of their lives to be the toughest on me physically and emotionally.

My two maternity leaves were each only six weeks. When I resumed working, it was challenging to juggle deadlines, conference calls, or meetings as well as their feeding patterns. My sleep requirements were the last item on my agenda. It was an exhausting time, one I do not wish to resume with another baby.

Currently I feel it would be great to get some more sleep, but then I would not be able to accomplish the tasks that need to get done by certain dates. For example, my PR business comes first before writing this book, so I've been writing this book at night and on the weekends, when I could be relaxing by reading a novel or watching television.

I sometimes crave coffee in the afternoon if I am feeling sluggish. If I have a cup of java at 2 p.m., this keeps me awake until midnight or later. Fortunately, my two toddlers will usually sleep through the night. Yet they do wake occasionally before dawn, and I will have to see what is going on.

As working moms with young kids, you have to become an early riser. There is no choice. You are always on call, like a doctor is on call for her patients. If you don't get the necessary sleep you need, then your health and mood may suffer as a result

– and this will invariably affect the home front.

Some moms shared with me the sleep issues they were currently facing. Adrienne Noel, CEO of Marketing Minds At Work, a marketing and advertising agency in Central Florida, said she doesn't have enough time in the day to do everything she needs to do. Noel works long hours as a business owner and is the single parent of a 4-year-old who deserves her attention when she is around, Noel said. Less sleep has not affected her work. Fortunately, her schedule is flexible enough where she can take a nap if she's really tired.

'The only real issue with less sleep (for her) is that it translates into more awake hours which leaves more time to eat,' Noel confided. 'Invariably, I'm hungry through the night, so I eat sandwiches, ice cream, and other munchies. I've put on some weight over the last year.'

Noel is self-employed, but the economic downturn hasn't been much of a problem for her. However, she admitted because her sleeping pattern is really disjointed, she would probably have a tough time resuming a regular sleeping pattern, were she to rejoin Corporate America. She is not sure whether she could get to the office at 8 a.m. again.

Broken Sleep

For Laura Ellick, PhD, a New York state-licensed psychologist, the biggest challenge of having kids is the broken (or interrupted) sleep and the lack of a consistent eight to nine hours at one time. She says that even seven hours would be good sometimes. 'Prior to having kids, I was an eight- to nine-hour-a-night kind of gal – I never pulled an all-nighter, even in college, because I just do not function well without a full night of sleep.'

Unfortunately, none of Ellick's kids was a good sleeper as a baby. In fact, her now 9-year-old son didn't sleep through the night until he started kindergarten. 'In addition, they are early risers, so we would all be up at 5 a.m.,' she said. 'Because of the nature of my work, I went back to work about one week after having each of my kids – so to say I was tired was an understatement.'

Ellick cried at work many days because she was so tired, and she wondered how she was going to get through the day. She had difficulties concentrating and being able to work effectively. 'In addition, sleep deprivation makes me very cranky and emotional, so I had to work twice as hard to keep things in check. I wound up closing my door many times, putting my feet on the desk, and trying to take a nap. I have even tried to nap in my car during lunch hour,' she admitted. 'To be honest, I kept my work schedule to the barest of part-time, because I knew I didn't have the stamina to work more than a couple of days a week. My immune system also crashes when I don't sleep, so I spent a lot more time being sick, too.'

Ellick told me she has worked around the sleep issue as best as she can. 'I have altered my work schedule so that I can take a nap before I go to work (she works until 8 p.m. sometimes) so I can make it through the day. I have also slept on my children's bedroom floor, in their beds, or wherever else I was needed so that I could calm a child down and try to get some sleep too. I used to be able to get through the day with just a morning cup of coffee, but I now need an afternoon jolt as well,' she said. 'I also just remind myself when I am up with a crying or sick child that biology will eventually take over, and they will fall asleep in the end. Sometimes just reminding myself that the human body will take over is enough to relax me and get me through – I can see the light at the end of the tunnel.'

Christa Carr, a communications expert based in New York City, said she will take advantage when all are asleep to catch up on emails. Carr also runs her own PR business, with a 4-year-old and eight-month-old to look after. She is exhausted and confided she will be up by 6 a.m. with the baby and 4-year-old. 'I allow myself two nights a week to stay up late like I'm doing to catch up on all emails,' she wrote to me one evening after midnight.

On the one hand, Carr needs to be fresh which requires at least seven hours of sleep, but she also needs time alone to work – so her sleep is often sacrificed in order to keep up with her work. Like me and many women with whom I spoke, she also works on weekends.

Carr feels her lack of quality sleep time has affected her work. 'I literally missed an email from my client saying I should be paid more! I just didn't see it as I was tired and only later on – about two weeks later – I was going through old emails, and I saw the message. I could not believe it,' she admitted. 'If I don't get enough sleep I can "blank" on things; I think I'm fully awake, but actually I'm not thinking properly and can miss important details in work.'

Carr prepares her weeks carefully. 'For days I need to be sharp, when I'm doing critical work, I make sure I go to bed early – "sleep is a weapon" and, in the end, it is better to be well rested and behind in work than sleep deprived and making mistakes,' she said. 'Still, as tonight is an example, I have to catch up on emails, and this means sacrificing sleep. So for days with meetings I go to bed early the night before, and days with analytical work I go to bed early.'

Carr is feeling the strain of the economic downturn. She is doing far more work, for less pay (by 50 percent less and no benefits), and she's working her hardest ever to keep her clients happy. She doesn't have much time for downtime. 'I am constantly thinking I should be doing something for them or might miss something. There is fierce competition so I need to work very hard and demand is greater than ever,' she concluded. 'My clients even call me on weekends and in the evening. I work harder now than I ever did when I was working for a corporation.' She did corporate work for ten years before she had children and started her freelance work. Carr has also started to drink a lot of coffee, which she thinks is probably not good for her health.

Exercise Is Critical

Jennifer Dominiquini, a marketing executive and blog writer at frontlinemom.com, knows how challenging managing a full schedule, a full-time job, and two young children can be. Luckily, her husband Daniel decided to stay at home with the kids, making it more possible for her to balance the many demands in her life. 'However, when my second child was born in 2010, I was just five months into a busy new job. The typical demands and stresses of being a new mom, a demanding job, and dealing with the excitement but at times jealousy of my first child did not allow for much free time,' Dominiquini said. 'Our relatives live far away, so getting even just a little break proved to be challenging. This lack of slack, coupled with the lack of sleep caused by an adorable infant who refused to sleep for long stretches at time, could have meant disaster.'

Falling asleep or taking it easy at the job was no option for Dominiquini. 'In the past I have used exercise to relieve stress and minimize sleepiness. However, with two kids and a new job, sticking to my exercise routine was almost impossible. I was frustrated and stuck in a rut. Then I got some advice that woke me up, literally. While exerting myself on a work-related project, I had the opportunity to talk with a personal trainer who gave me solid advice.'

The trainer told Dominiquini that even if she exercises for only ten minutes in the morning or evening, this is better than nothing. 'You will feel better,' was the promise. 'Make the effort to exercise even when you would much rather curl up on the couch and loaf,' was the rallying cry.

'So, I started. Little by little I got running again, in 5, 10, 15 minutes increments at a time. I bought a treadmill to make it easier to deal with the inclement Chicago weather and I stuck with it, little by little,' Dominiquini said. 'This minor shift in my routine made all the difference. Each bit of exercise refreshed me and made me more able to tackle the many demands in mind.

Even the middle-of-the-night feedings didn't feel so challenging anymore.'

Getting Required Sleep

With the helpful, but anecdotal advice from moms, I turned to the experts and asked, 'How can working mothers with babies or toddlers get the sleep they need?'

- Meeta Singh, MD, a sleep specialist at Henry Ford Hospital in Detroit, said the sleep cycle is still developing in a newborn for the first year of life. 'Typically, a newborn will sleep for short periods over 24 hours. When awake, they need to be fed and changed. So the sleep cycle of a new mother is disrupted,' Singh said. 'Initially, one way to combat this sleep deprivation would be to nap during the day when the baby naps. However, once the mother is back at work, then this sleep deprivation is a big issue.'

  'As long as the baby is waking at night, the mother may need assistance from her spouse or other family member to help with at least one night feeding. This will protect a few hours of uninterrupted sleep,' Singh advised. 'Taking a short 15 to 20 minute power nap at work (if possible) can also help. Protecting bedtimes and making sure that one goes to bed early enough at night are other ways to achieve your required sleep.'

  As the infant grows and starts sleeping through the night, Singh recommends that the mother goes to bed in a timely fashion. Also, keep the sleep environment cool and dimly lit. Finally, Singh said we're all aware that when infants grow up to be teenagers, and young adults, they may still disrupt their mother's sleep in multiple ways. (I wonder: Is 'Get used to it' a happy or helpful piece of advice?)

- Tracey Marks, MD, author of the book, *Master Your Sleep*

(Bascom Hill, 2011), said it's tough, no doubt. 'Typically, the solution to sleep disruptions due to lifestyle inter-ference is addressing the behaviors that interfere with sleep. In this case, the source of the problem (your infant) is not entirely within your control,' she said.

- Dr. Marcia Lindsey, a clinical psychologist and sleep coach based in Houston, said it may be next to impossible for moms of babies or toddlers to get the sleep they need. 'When your child is not yet on a regular sleep schedule, neither are you. The most important thing a mom can do is to try to keep as regular a schedule as possible,' she said. That may sound like contradictory advice, but here's what she means: Moms who have not slept and who are dragging through work the next day may be tempted to nap during the day or to go to bed early. This would be just the wrong thing to do to 'make up' sleep.

'What sleep we lose on a given night just increases our sleep drive for the next night. We should sleep better the next night after a bad night because of that,' Lindsey said. 'When we alter our normal sleep schedule too much, we lose the pattern of going to sleep easily and staying asleep. Moms can end up having trouble getting to sleep at all. Another reason to keep the same bedtimes and rising times is that we are also training our child how to sleep. If they can learn to sleep well, then we will get more sleep.'

Today's Sleep Challenges

What are the main sleep challenges working mothers are facing right now? According to Marks, it's having too many obligations and responsibilities. 'A typical working mom can face another job when she returns home in the evening with cooking, cleaning, baths, homework, and so forth. If she has a job that doesn't end at 5 p.m., then she can bring work home that she has to continue after everyone else has gone to bed,' Marks said. 'So I find that sleep problems seen in working moms are from going to bed late or having trouble falling asleep due to stress.'

Owing to the level of their responsibilities, working moms are challenged just to get enough quality sleep. 'When job and family responsibilities mount, it is tempting for moms to sacrifice sleep for something else they may have to do. When sleep becomes shortened, we have much less energy to meet those responsibilities because sleep has such an effect on our daytime functioning,' Lindsey said. 'Daytime fatigue is common for working moms with young children.'

Another sleep challenge is getting regular, quality sleep. Insomnia is rampant today, and women are especially prone to poor sleep, not only from the additional stress of their multifaceted lives but also from their unique hormonal events, Lindsey added.

Sleep is both affected by hormone changes and, in turn, affects them. 'Sleep is part of what repairs the hormone system and re-balances the hormones each night. Disruptions in sleep can increase cortisol, the stress hormone, and may also affect thyroid, estrogen, progesterone, and testosterone in women,' Lindsey said. 'In addition, stress has a direct effect on the hormones that allow us to get to sleep and stay asleep.'

According to the National Sleep Foundation, the main sleep challenges that affect working mothers are as follows:

1. In a 24-hour society with work, social, and family demands, what usually gets cut is the time spent in bed.
2. Shift workers – about one in five Americans – work non-traditional hours (not the typical hours of 9 a.m. to 5 p.m.). Difficulty falling asleep is a common effect, as is obtaining quality sleep during the day. Women who work on the night shift get less sleep and have more disrupted sleep. Shift workers, in general, report more sleep-related accidents and illnesses. Night and rotating shifts can put a

strain on a family, when less time is available to meet family or home responsibilities as well as enjoy recreational and social activities. Female shift workers also suffer irregular menstrual cycles, difficulty getting pregnant, higher rates of miscarriage, premature births, and low birth-weight babies more than regular day-working women, according to several large studies. Still, most shift-working women do have normal, healthy babies. Changes in exposure to light, and lost sleep caused by shift work, may have biological or hormonal effects that are not yet entirely understood. One large study of women who worked night shifts over a three-year period found a 60 percent greater risk for developing breast cancer. Female shift workers should consult their doctors if they experience menstrual difficulties, infertility, pregnancy or other medical conditions.

3. An estimated 18 million Americans have sleep apnea. While apnea is more common in men, it increases in women after age 50. Since being overweight is a risk factor for sleep apnea, the increase in abdominal fat during menopause may be one reason menopausal women are 3.5 times as likely to get this sleep disorder. Some attribute the prevalence to hormonal changes such as the decrease in progesterone. Studies have also found that sleep apnea is associated with increased blood pressure, a risk for cardio-vascular disease, and stroke. If any of these symptoms appear, it is important to seek a doctor's help.

4. Insomnia is secondary to various life, work, or family stressors. Women are more likely than men to report insomnia. In fact, according to the 2002 National Science Foundation (NSF) Sleep in America poll, more women than men experience symptoms of insomnia at least a few nights a week (63 percent vs. 54 percent) and they are more likely to have daytime sleepiness. Sometimes, women

begin to have sleepless nights associated with menstruation, pregnancy, or menopause, and find it difficult to break poor sleep habits.

5. Women, especially women with children, have a greater incidence of restless legs syndrome (RLS) that might disrupt sleep. In the NSF 2002 Sleep in America poll, 18 percent of the female adult population reported RLS symptoms a few nights a week or more. Due to difficulties sleeping, RLS can lead to daytime sleepiness, mood swings, anxiety, and depression. One study found that 42 percent of those with RLS stated that it affected their relationship with their partner.

6. More women (58 percent) suffer from nighttime pain than men (48 percent), according to a 1996 NSF Gallup Poll. In a more recent 2000 NSF Sleep in America poll, one in four women reported that pain or physical discomfort interrupted their sleep three nights a week or more.

Economic Effect

'The current economy affects women's sleep in different ways. Women are now working longer hours. They may have to travel a longer distance to get to work, which may involve waking up earlier or coming home later in the evening and thus getting to bed late,' Singh said. 'Additionally the associated stress can precipitate insomnia, resulting in difficulty initiating or maintaining sleep.'

The economic downturn has required more than a few women to return to work to help the family finances or, if already employed, to work more hours. In this case, Marks said the woman who returned to work now has more on her plate to deal with. Another possibility is the woman who is the primary breadwinner and who manages the family finances. 'This woman may have trouble sleeping because of the additional pressure of making ends meet as well as taking care of the family. Worrying about finances is traditionally the man's role in two-parent families, but more and more working women take on the burden of family finances in addition to bearing the lion's share of home responsibilities,' she said. 'In the traditional situation where the man is the breadwinner, he typically is relieved of having to attend to home tasks and, in fact, may come home to dinner waiting and the kids tucked away by a wife who may or may not have a job as well.'

Anything which causes worry and anxiety can affect our sleep. 'One of the classic reasons for not being able to get to sleep is not being able to turn off the noise in our brains. The damaged economy is certainly affecting everyone's financial picture and also their sense of well-being,' Lindsey said. 'Women are feeling stressed about their job security and their potential future income, which often leads to sleep challenges. For those women who are more sensitive to anxious concerns, sleep is one of the first places to be affected.'

Health Effects

Just how serious is chronic sleep deprivation? Prolonged sleep deprivation increases the risk of suffering from a stroke or heart disease, according to a major long-term study published in February 2011 based on the experiences of hundreds of thousands of people across eight countries. The trend for late nights and early mornings was described as a ticking time bomb by the researchers at the University of Warwick, who linked a lack of sleep to a range of disorders which often result in early death.

Chronic short sleep produces in the body hormones and chemicals, which increase the risk of developing heart disease, strokes, and other conditions such as high blood pressure and cholesterol, diabetes, and obesity, according to Dr. Michelle Miller of the University of Warwick.

Miller and Professor Francesco Cappuccio, who co-authored

a report published in the *European Heart Journal*, followed up evidence spanning seven to twenty-five years from more than 470,000 participants across eight countries, including Japan, the US, Sweden, and the UK.

Cappuccio concluded if you sleep less than six hours per night, and if you have disturbed sleep, then you garner a 48 percent greater chance of developing or dying from heart disease and a 15 percent greater chance of developing or dying from a stroke. The trend for late nights and early mornings is a ticking time bomb for our health – so you need to act now to reduce your risk of developing these life-threatening conditions.

'There is an expectation in today's society to fit more into our lives. The whole work-life balance struggle is causing too many of us to trade in precious sleeping time to ensure we complete all the jobs we believe are expected of us. But, in doing so, we are significantly increasing the risk of suffering a stroke or developing cardiovascular disease resulting in, for example, heart attacks,' Cappuccio added.

These are alarming stats which made me ponder what I can do to change my current work-life balance so my physical health is not compromised. A trip to my doctor this week for abdominal pain made me realize just how important it is to not neglect your own health. When you don't feel well, you can't take time off because you have kids to drop off and pick up at school, food shopping and cooking to do, and all the rest – in addition to work deadlines. The busy schedule does not slow down when you do.

Perhaps I need to hire a babysitter during the week for Emma when she is not in daycare so I can finish more work during the day. This would allow me to have some down time at night so I could relax a bit and spend time off the computer.

A good question to ask yourself is: What can I do differently so I can get more quality sleep time and relaxation? Can you eliminate the afternoon coffee? Can you break away at lunch to exercise at the gym? Can you fit in more time to read novels at night rather than catch up on paperwork?

Singh offered these proper sleep tips for stressed-out career moms:

1. Avoid television, working on computers or smart phones close to bedtime, and don't check your phone in the middle of the night.
2. Avoid alcohol too close to bedtime.
3. Avoid strenuous exercise too close to bedtime.
4. Avoid caffeinated products close to bedtime.

Marks had these suggestions for today's multitasking women:

• Eliminate unnecessary/non-required commitments. Since babies and toddlers consume a lot of time, understand that you will not be able to do all of the other things you used to. This includes keeping the house showroom ready.
• Hire help with tasks that don't require you. This would include tasks like house cleaning and cooking.
• If you have a toddler, be vigilant about getting your toddler on a regular sleep schedule. Poorly sleeping kids means sleep-deprived parents.
• If you have a baby, it's even more important to accept that for a limited period of time, you will not be as productive as you once were. That is, take naps when your baby sleeps and don't use that time to get things accomplished. Even though broken sleep is not as restorative as continuous sleep, the infant stage is a time to maximize naps in order to get as much sleep as possible in a 24-hour period.

In closing, it's important to know your own body, which will tell you if you're not getting enough daily sleep or relaxation. You want to avoid getting to a point where you feel completely burnt out – this may lead to a long-term physical condition or worst-case scenario, heart disease or a stroke. Bottom line – get enough sleep yourself so you can care for your precious loved ones!

Chapter 6

Nutrition: How Do I Ensure My Family Eats Healthily?

For many working mothers, the meal preparation time at day's end is demanding. After a long day at the office or being stuck in traffic, the last thing you may want to do is cook dinner. Is this situation common in your household some nights? You try to prepare a meal while watching your toddler, but the human interactions do not go as smoothly as you had pictured. You fight fatigue while you burn the chicken, load the dishwasher, and try to get your two-year-old to stop howling for your attention or bothering the cat.

Evenings in our household can sometime be challenging. Jason loves to cook, but is particular about how meals are prepared. As a result, he will often cook our meals and freeze half of the production for a later date. My friends think I am crazy to mention it because it seems wonderful to them having a spouse who takes over as the 'top chef.' Yet some nights, in place of reheating leftovers, I would love the chance to experiment with my own favorite dishes. Instead, I have become the relief cook or the pinch hitter – scrambling to whip up dinner at 5:30 p.m. when I should have prepared it ahead of time. Question is, when would I have had time to do that?

I was curious to know how other busy career mothers handled the dinner situation and the meal issues with which they struggled. A few working moms shared with me how they ensure their families eat healthy meals when they are time pressed to food shop and cook.

Shannon Miller remains the most decorated American gymnast in history. Miller is the only American to rank among the all-time top ten gymnasts and the only female athlete to be inducted into the US Olympics Hall of Fame twice (individual, 2006; and team, 2008). Miller has made it her mission to help other women achieve a healthy and fit lifestyle. In 2011, after a diagnosis of a germ cell tumor – a type of ovarian cancer – she has become a passionate advocate for women to get their exams and screenings on a regular basis. Shannon and her husband welcomed their first child, John Rocco, in October 2009.

'Whether it's chasing my 2-year-old, running to meetings, or just keeping up with life, it's difficult to focus on healthy eating. It's important to be prepared. I look for those pockets of time when I'm already preparing food to prepare a little extra,' Miller told me. 'I can freeze the extras or prepare snacks and meals that will be ready to grab from the refrigerator. Overall, I try to keep the driving to a minimum by grouping activities together. Instead of running across town for one item, I keep a list of "to-dos" so that I can group them together for the most efficient use of my time.'

Can Miller relate to the end-of-day meal preparation struggle? 'Absolutely!' she told me. 'Some people love to cook. It gives them an outlet for stress release. Not me. I want to get it going and get it finished. The last thing I want to do when I come home from a long day of filming or meetings is get stuck in the kitchen cooking and cleaning,' said Miller. 'There are days that my husband and I spend a little more time, talking and preparing a meal, but for the most part we'd rather be playing with our son than slaving over a stove.'

Advance Preparation

Miller looks for meals that are easy to prepare in advance and that she can pop in the oven. 'We also love "salad bar" nights. I chop everything up in advance, we use leftover chicken from grilling on the weekend, and we set everything out on the counter. Everyone gets exactly what they want and it's a good healthy meal that's easy to clean up (just pop the lids back on the plasticware) and get on with life!' Miller confided.

Any nutrition lessons learned over the years? 'I wouldn't say I avoid fast food all together; I've just learned what to order. Sometimes the drive-thru is about all you can handle. If you are having one of those days, understand that all is not lost,' Miller admitted. 'Ordering a plain baked potato with grilled chicken is a good option. For kids, most fast food chains now have fresh-fruit options, if you need a quick snack. The biggest lesson I've learned is an everything-in-moderation approach. I don't cut out complete foods or food groups, but I do watch my portion size and try to get a variety of food each day.'

Daytime Emmy-nominated actress Alicia Minshew is best known for portraying Kendall Hart on the daytime drama *All My Children*. In October 2008, Minshew married Richie Herschenfeld, a New York City restaurant owner, who is also the best friend of her on-screen husband Thorsten Kaye. Minshew and her husband welcomed the birth of their daughter Willow Lenora Herschenfeld in November 2009. Minshew went on maternity leave right as *All My Children* relocated production to Los Angeles.

'My hubby is the cook of the household most of the time. We cook a lot of our organic veggie and meat dishes, and freeze them. So – if we are in a bind – we can just defrost, heat up, and are ready to go!' Minshew said.

She can relate to the evening scramble for a meal. 'When my hubby is out of town tending to his restaurants, I do relate to that struggle. That is why we plan our meals ahead and cook in bulk (like stews and chilis). This way we have meals for the baby for days!' Minshew said.

What nutrition lessons has Minshew gleaned? 'Avoid junk food for sure! Get your child used to eating healthily early – like my mom did for me. Instead of candy – give fruit. Instead of cookies – try yogurt or dry cereal. They can eat healthily from day one, if you teach them!'

Paige Wolf, Philadelphia-based author of *Spit That Out: The Overly Informed Parent's Guide to Raising Children in the Age of Environmental Guilt* (Lombard Books, 2010), told me that subscribing to a community-supported agriculture share forces her to be creative and find ways to use fresh fruits and veggies. 'To always have healthy snacks on hand, I love making popsicles – just use a hand blender to mix whatever fruit and veggie you have and stick them into ice pop molds. Kids love them, and they are a great low-cal snack for mom,' Wolf said. 'Crock pots are always a go-to, especially in the winter. Throw things in before you leave for work, and when you get home you have a great slow-cooked meal.'

Wolf said she is lucky to work mostly from home, so she has the advantage of being close to the stove. 'But I know many moms don't have that luxury and convenience, and I imagine it would be much harder if you don't get home until later in the evening. A few full-time working moms I know have a Sunday tradition – they spend part of the day cooking meals for the week so everything is prepared, often frozen for days,' she said. 'Personally, I make big batches of pasta sauce and vegetable soup, and freeze them in portions for easy use whenever we need them. I think one of my biggest fears is the power going out long enough to defrost all my hard work in the freezer!'

Her lessons learned? 'My toddler refuses to eat almost anything but pizza and cookies. Fortunately, he is accustomed to healthy PB+Js – unsweetened organic peanut butter and jam on wholegrain bread. I fear the day he sees another kid with soft white bread and processed peanut butter, and begs to switch!' Wolf told me. 'But I have accepted pizza once a week, and I have even let him have McDonald's fries a couple times. I recognize that it's the patterns that count, and a few glitches along the way won't determine his overall eating habits.'

The Downturn's Effect

The economic downturn has forced many working mothers to cut back on critical food purchases for their families. One in six people in America is going to bed hungry, and one in five families live at or below the poverty line. While food prices are rising, wages are clearly not. In March 2011, CNN Money reported that food prices in the US are rising once again, due to growing demand and tight supplies of wheat, corn, and other key commodities. American consumers are seeing higher grocery bills when gas prices are at an all-time high. According to the US government's Consumer Price Index, food prices in January 2011 rose 1.8 percent from the prior year, marking the fastest pace since 2009.

Healthy eating on the cheap, believe it or not, is possible, according to Jaime Bakoss, CHHC, AADP, certified nutrition counselor and owner of Harmony Holistic Nutrition in Atlanta. 'When I'm giving health-food-store tours, one of my favorite sections to introduce my clients to is the bulk aisle – most people avoid it because they don't know what to do with food that doesn't come in boxes, bags, and other packaging, but this aisle is the land of real savings!' Bakoss said. 'For instance, at Whole Foods, you can buy two cups of brown rice (equals eight servings) or two cups of protein-rich quinoa (equals eight servings) for a few dollars. These nutrient-dense grains make fantastic side dishes and are loaded with vitamins and minerals.'

Dried beans are also inexpensive, and a great source of protein and dietary fiber. 'You can buy a couple cups of chickpeas for a few bucks and make your own hummus, or add them to salads and stir-fries for an extra nutritional boost. I also teach my clients how to make more snacks for themselves and their kids – it's a great way to eliminate the preservatives, artificial colors, and overly processed ingredients in many popular snack foods, plus it's a big money-saver,' Bakoss told me. 'In the bulk aisle, you can pick up oats, nuts, seeds, dried fruit, and coconut flakes for homemade granola, breakfast bars, trail mixes, nut butters, raw truffles, and lots of other treats.'

'The produce aisle is obviously the most important section – spend most of your time there,' Bakoss said. 'Look for seasonal, local produce – that's usually the least expensive and the most nutritious and environmentally friendly since it had to travel the least amount of miles to reach the store. Many people (I know because I used to be one of them!) spend too much money on superfoods and supplements boasting mega antioxidants and vitamins,' she continued. 'Forget these pricey and expertly marketed products, and buy some kale, collards, watercress, cabbage, root veggies, mushrooms, squashes, berries, apples, peaches, berries – whatever is in season! Feel good knowing that your body is getting the nourishment it needs for that particular time of year.'

Nutritious Foods Are Vital

Erin Macdonald, RD, nutrition, fitness, and wellness coach and co-founder of U Rock Girl, agrees that some of the most nutritious foods are actually the least expensive ones. 'The stuff in packages, such as cookies, chips, crackers, cupcakes, "kid-friendly" snack foods, actually cost the most,' she said.

Macdonald's advice for eating healthily on a budget:

- Get back to the basics – fresh fruit and vegetables, whole grains (brown rice, quinoa, old-fashioned oats), corn tortillas, sweet potatoes, and beans.
- Watch the sales – when your market has chicken breasts on sale, buy them and buy extra to freeze for later.
- If you can cut out the expensive 'snack' foods (which are highly processed and low in nutritional value), put some of that money toward organic dairy (milk, yogurt, cheese) as it's so important to give kids hormone-free foods. The same is true with purchasing organic produce for the 'dirty

dozen': apples, peaches, strawberries, lettuce, celery, spinach, nectarines (imported), grapes (imported), sweet bell peppers, potatoes, blueberries (domestic US), and kale or collard greens.

- Buy in bulk wherever you can for grains, nuts, and cereal. Nuts should be kept refrigerated to keep them from going rancid due to their high fat content. Keep whole grains in well-sealed containers for freshness.

- Keep bags of frozen fruit and vegetables on hand at all times. All you have to do is toss a bag of frozen veggies in the microwave, oven, or into a large wok for a quick stir-fry to ensure that every dinner has vegetables.

- Do your fresh vegetables go bad in the refrigerator and get thrown away before they get eaten? Frozen veggies are just as nutritious as fresh, as they are picked at the peak of ripeness and immediately washed and frozen to lock in their nutrition. Canned veggies are just as nutritious, but are usually too high in sodium and often don't have the same pleasant texture as frozen (or fresh).

- Buy dried herbs and spices in small quantities. It may seem like such a good deal to buy them in larger bottles, but most people do not get through a bottle fast enough. Their shelf life is 6 to 12 months. Better yet, learn how to cook with lots of spices, which is the trick to making every meal more delicious. That way, you use up those spices in a timely fashion, and they remain fresh and flavorful.

Ling Wong, MS, CHHC, AADP, a nutrition and wellness coach based in Santa Monica, runs two businesses and has a toddler at home. 'I usually have 30 to 45 minutes to cook while my husband does the bedtime story with my son. I need to set up my cooking and my kitchen "operation" to be systematic and efficient,' Wong said. 'I always feel like there isn't enough time. And I feel somewhat guilty when I have to do "frozen" once in a while...

but I always make a point of including a healthy serving of fresh vegetables in every meal.'

I personally find myself going to the supermarket too frequently during the week – there always ends up being some new items I need to purchase for the kids or we run out of something crucial like orange juice, milk or bananas. If I spent less time at the supermarket, I could spend this time cooking.

Wong advised there are a few ways to make shopping and cooking less time-consuming:

- Do all the shopping in one trip during the weekend and block out a couple of hours to cook four to five meals that you can put in the fridge or freezer for the workweek.
- Cook once, eat twice: cook enough so you can split the food into two meals.
- Cook a big batch of whole grain, and use it in different ways: For example, cook one big batch of brown rice. First night serve with stir fry, second night make a fried rice, and then make a brown rice porridge for breakfast (variations: for savory, add vegetable, peanut, soy sauce, egg; for sweet, add cinnamon, honey/maple or rice syrup, banana, apple sauce or raisin).
- Team up with four to five other families. Each family prepares one dish enough for all, and then trade – now you have five dishes for every night of the week!
- It's okay to use frozen meals once in a while – in fact, have a few healthy ones handy. Make sure you pick healthy choices (read the label, avoid added sugar, too much sodium, chemicals, and additives), and make a point of including a decent side portion of fresh produce (salad, sautéed spinach, grilled zucchini).

Wong's nutrition lessons include:

- Read labels for everything. Watch out for chemicals, additives, and added sugar (which is present in many packaged foods, even savory ones). Reduce caffeine – again, watch out for energy drinks and soft drinks.
- Definitely avoid fast foods – they are high in sugar and usually contain many chemicals.
- Cultivate mindful eating. Eat sitting down, chew slowly and thoroughly, appreciate your foods, and avoid eating on the run. Sharing a meal with the family is a great way to cultivate mindful eating and to enjoy food.
- Stay hydrated to curb cravings.

Being a working mom and a nutrition counselor, Bakoss is always looking for new ways to cook healthy food – quickly – for her family. 'Meal planning and prepping are, by far, my best options. My clients often tell me that my meal plans are their favorite parts of my programs. They're key to gaining a little extra weeknight time,' Bakoss said. 'Just create a rough outline of breakfasts, lunches, and dinners for five days and a corresponding grocery list. The outline will not only shorten grocery-shopping time, but it will eliminate the last-minute "What do we do for dinner tonight?" dilemma. I like to meal plan a day or two before I do my Sunday food shopping, so my whole day doesn't revolve around meal planning, shopping, and preparing meals.'

Here are Bakoss' nutrition tips for working moms:

- If you are dealing with an unusually overwhelming week, you can recycle an old meal plan. Also, trade meal plans with friends for more ideas.
- Use up the more perishable produce (leafy greens, berries) in the beginning of the week and save meals with heartier produce (root veggies, cabbage, squashes, apples, pears) for the end of the week.
- If you are making grains like quinoa or brown rice, then

make sure you can use them in a few different meals. For instance, you could use brown rice or quinoa in

- A sweet, warm breakfast bowl (warm cooked grains with milk or milk alternative, cinnamon, a bit of maple syrup, raisins, and topped with walnuts)
- A soup or chili or stew
- A 'taco-less' rice, bean, veggie bowl
- A side dish by adding dried fruit, seeds, fresh herbs, and an olive oil and lemon dressing

- Likewise, if you cook a bunch of beans, make sure you have a few different opportunities to utilize them:
  - Make a bean dip
  - Add them to salads, pastas, and grain dishes
- If you're buying a whole chicken, then have roasted chicken one night, use leftovers for chicken salad for lunch, and use the bones for a soup stock.

Spend more time with your kids by getting them involved with the meal planning, too. 'Have them pick a meal for which they will help shop and then prepare. Even if your children are young, they can choose a pink, green, or purple smoothie for breakfast or a snack and help find the appropriate fruits and veggies,' Bakoss advised.

Once you have your meals planned and your groceries bought, it is time to prepare some meals and snacks for the week. Pick one night as prep night. Sundays usually work best for Bakoss. 'I like to prep alone; I turn on the iPod, drink a glass of wine or a cup of tea, and start cooking! It's a really meditative, wonderful time for me, and many of my clients have said that they're surprised at how good it feels to work in their kitchens,' she said. 'I don't make all the meals for the week. I cook up a pot or two of grains (quinoa, millet, brown rice, and buckwheat are my staples), a pot of beans (lentils, chickpeas, white beans, or black beans), and I wash, chop, and dry my greens (kale, collards, arugula, swiss chard, spinach, romaine – whatever's in season).'

Bakoss tries to make a new dip for their veggie sticks and a homemade salad dressing during this time too. 'It sounds like a lot, but once the grains and beans are on the stove you don't have to do anything with them until the timer goes off, so while they're cooking, I'm preparing other food. In less than two hours, nourishing meals for the busy week are prepped,' she said. 'I save the snack foods and treats (muffins, granola, raisin bars, raw chocolate balls) to make with my son one day after school. If my grains and veggies are mostly prepared for the week, the protein component is the only thing I need to concentrate on for dinner, which usually cooks pretty quickly. Breakfasts are ready in about 5 minutes, lunches are packed in about 5 to 10 minutes, and dinners are ready in less than 15 minutes.'

As for animal-based products, Bakoss' best advice is to eat the highest quality meat, poultry, pork, fish, eggs, or dairy products possible because grass-fed or pastured-raised animals have loads more Omega 3s, CLAs, vitamins, and minerals (and significantly less saturated fat and cholesterol) than their conventional counterparts – but they're pricey. 'Eat less of them and more plant-based proteins. There's no reason to eat animal food at every meal or even every day,' she concluded. 'Experiment and see what works best for your body.'

Smart Planning

Macdonald said it all boils down to planning. 'Plan a week's worth of meals out on a Saturday or Sunday. From that menu, one can make a comprehensive marketing list. Then go to the market and purchase only those necessary ingredients,' she advised. 'Once home, take one to two hours to prepare as many dishes as possible and refrigerate or freeze them for use later in the week. Then when it's time for dinner, all you have to do is reheat. It's best to plan dinner items in which one or two can be prepared on the stove while one or two dishes are in the oven at the same time.'

One of the best kitchen investments you could make is in a slow cooker (such as registered brand, Crock Pot). Jason loves to make beef stew and bean soup in our slow cooker. He will make huge pots and freeze half of it so we have some back-up meals. These frozen meals come in handy when schedules change or the weather is stormy. 'It's such a great tool because you just put in all of your ingredients in the morning, set it to cook for six to ten hours and when you get home, everything is ready. It's so simple,' Macdonald agreed.

While those meals are cooking away, do as much snack prep work as possible. Macdonald suggested that moms:

- Cut up veggies and put them in reusable containers or zip-top bags so they are ready to eat for an after-school snack.
- Go one step further and make a whole bunch of cut-up veggies or edamame (soy beans), loading them into snack-size zip-top bags. Then, when you are packing up your food for the work or school day, it is just grab-and-go.
- Make individual snack-size baggies of nuts or homemade trail mix (cereal, nuts, and dried fruit).
- Place a large bowl of fruit on the kitchen counter or table (prominently displayed). When kids come home from school and want a snack, this option is staring them in the face. Just as 'out of sight is out of mind,' so in sight seems to be in mind. Fill the bowl with apples, pears, oranges, tangerines, bananas, peaches, nectarines, plums – all fruits that don't have to be refrigerated. Choose fruit that is both seasonal and local. Keep cut-up chunks of melon or bunches of grapes ready to go in the refrigerator.
- Keep bags of frozen fruit in the freezer, especially for fruit that is not in season (like berries in the winter). Great for making smoothies or just thaw and include in your meal.
- Moms should pack a cooler (or insulated but stylish bag)

full of healthy and tasty snacks and water for when they are on the go all day long. Make sure to fill your cooler with a variety of fruits and veggies as well as protein, like string cheese, yogurt (preferably nonfat Greek-style), hard-boiled eggs, edamame, nuts, or sliced turkey. Being prepared for hungry children (and mom, too) will keep you from driving through the drive-thru at the local fast food establishment or entering the local convenience store or ice cream parlor.

Macdonald shared some final expert tips:

- Let the kids help make the menu for the week. Each child should be able to choose the dinner for at least one night of the week and should choose one protein, one whole grain, at least one vegetable, and one fruit. That way the meal is nice and balanced.
- Think about colors and 'eat the colors of the rainbow' to ensure a high level of nutrition for each meal. Aim for at least two colors of fruits/vegetables at each meal.
- Do recipe research on sites such as cooking.com, eatingwell.com, cookinglight.com, foodnetwork.com, epicurious.com, and vegetariantimes.com, as many of these recipes are prepared with a more health-conscious approach.
- Get the kids involved! Not only does it teach them an important lifelong skill but it also gives busy moms a much-needed helping hand (or two).

Writing this chapter made me realize I should spend more time researching the topic of nutritious meals. Even though Jason is an excellent cook, I would benefit from working individually with a local nutrition coach. I will add this to my to-do list.

In closing, some good questions to ask yourself: Are you

preparing healthy foods for your family? If not, what is preventing you from doing so – perceived lack of time, slimmer budget? What tips from this chapter will you implement to create healthier meals for the family? How can you save time on food shopping and meal preparation?

Bon Appetit!

Part 3

Parenting Issues

Chapter 7

Parenting: How Do I Overcome Challenging Issues?

Numerous challenges arise while caring for babies and toddlers. When I talk to working mothers at the park or play areas, the ones with older kids tell me, 'It gets easier when they're in school. When you can get past the breastfeeding and diaper duty, you're in good shape.' Certainly, when kids can dress and feed themselves, it gives mommies a bit of a break. I'm not at that stage yet.

Emma will be two years old in a few weeks. Kaitlyn will be four years old in a few months. Emma is still in diapers; we'll start potty training her soon. Kaitlyn still likes me to help dress her in the mornings. Emma likes to be spoon-fed her dinners. And of course, they are too young to bathe themselves.

Every month babies and toddlers change, and it's important for parents to be aware of major milestones and developments – to properly care for them as they grow. The book series *What to Expect* has been my Bible; I have checked it at various months in the girls' lives to read how to handle certain situations. *What to Expect the First Year* (Workman Publishing, 2003) was especially beneficial.

Deborah Gilman, PhD, licensed clinical psychologist and private practice psychologist in Pittsburgh, said women are more likely than men to flex their schedules to accommodate kids. This can be for simple things, such as getting the kids ready in the morning for daycare or school and picking the kids up after work. So from the moment mothers wake up, they feel the pressure of time – or lack thereof. Mothers feel a pull to be the best at work and the best at home. There is a difficulty in remaining balanced.

'Babies are certainly demanding, but I have found that many of the mothers in my practice also face the stressor of the lack of time they have to spend with their older school-aged children. It takes time to provide what children need – time to listen to the concerns they bring home, time to talk, check homework, time to have fun together or attend activities,' said Gilman.

Women struggle to structure business commitments and family commitments. Gilman's advice? Planning and organization can go a long way here – anticipating important events can reduce the push-pull feelings from both directions. Women with whom Gilman works have found it helpful to ask employers for flexible work arrangements, such as coming to work early on days when you need to leave early to attend a child's function or having every other Friday off.

Susan E. Caudle, PhD, ABPP, clinical psychologist, Texas Children's Hospital, and associate professor, Baylor College of Medicine, and a mom of two girls (ages 5 and 8), agreed that planning ahead has become required. 'My life is a logistical nightmare, and without a strong social network I'm not sure we would get everyone where they need to be on time. I'm a rather focused person. I prefer to work on one thing at a time. I've had to rework my personal style to one of constant multitasking. I've gotten better,' she said.

Caudle can make lunches for tomorrow while she makes dinner for tonight. She can rehearse spelling words on the way to soccer practice. She's more efficient at work so she can be home in time to get children to gymnastics. 'But this way of functioning isn't always comfortable, and I find it very draining. Maybe that's the main parenting issue – the working moms I know are tired all the time. This all sounds very negative and like I've given up a great deal. On the contrary, being a mom is the most rewarding thing I've ever done,' Caudle clarified. 'My kids are amazing and that's because of the work my husband and I have put in since day one. I expect great things from them, but they can't achieve without our support. So I'm tired. I also go to bed happy every night. I'll catch up on my sleep when they go to college.'

Economy Related Pressure

Several experts discussed how the economic downturn has put extra pressure on working mothers.

'Many women may not feel comfortable asking for flexible schedules or time off, for fear that they will be replaced by someone who does not need such accommodation. Employers may also be less inclined to allow flexible schedules, and working mothers may have to rely more on outside caregivers or their spouse for help with kids,' said Gilman. 'If the working mother is the sole provider for the household due to their spouse being unemployed, then added responsibility to provide for the family can bring added stress. Women may find it more difficult to achieve a healthy work-and-home balance if they feel the family is counting on her monetary input more than emotional input. Missing work to care for kids or even being stressed or overwhelmed may lead to reduced productivity and difficulty concentrating, requiring more work to be brought home at night or on weekends to catch up.'

Caudle thinks the economic situation has changed a lot of people's overall stress level. When we're stressed, we have less tolerance for frustration, less patience, and fewer emotional resources. 'This can render any parent vulnerable to using parenting strategies they might not normally employ. We know child abuse increases during times of economic hardship. This means all parents need to be particularly mindful of their emotional responses to child behavior,' she said. 'Getting over-the-top angry with your (albeit very frustrating) child rarely helps and often makes things worse. When you realize you are responding to bad behavior emotionally rather than rationally, step away. Tell your child you are angry and need a moment to get your thoughts together. Not only might you be avoiding doing something you'll regret later; you are also teaching your child great anger management skills by modeling them in real life.'

'When the parent is stressed, the child will know it and will act out more easily, more often, and more extremely,' said Jennifer Little, PhD, president of Parents Teach Kids, a firm that assesses children for learning problems and teaches parents how to effectively help their children. 'Economic stress usually brings adult yelling behaviors (fights and arguments) because the adults aren't dealing with their personal stress. The best solution for that? Parents need to have a date during which they can de-stress themselves and get back into the primary relationship (between them),' she said.

Children escalate those stress levels, especially when parents are tired from working and managing the home. 'Children know when parents feel guilt because parents give in more easily, are less consistent, and don't attend to them. Children just want parents' attention. If parents don't want the challenging behaviors, they need to spend time with the child – reading books, playing in the tub together, lying on the floor with blocks – instead of cleaning the house, making phone calls to friends or family, and so forth,' added Little.

Based on discussions with numerous other working mothers, these are some of the major challenges with which career moms have to deal: caring for sick babies, managing infant feeding schedules, and correcting toddler tantrums.

Caring for a Premature Baby

We have been fortunate to have been blessed with two healthy girls. Yet, I heard scary stories in which babies were born premature or ill and had to undergo surgery immediately. Mari Hancock, an executive at a communications agency, has a poignant story of caring for her premature baby while balancing work demands.

At about 25 weeks pregnant, Hancock was having severe headaches – to the point where she couldn't get out of bed. She continued to have terrible headaches and nausea; her doctor wasn't concerned. At 29 weeks, Hancock had a seizure, went into a coma, and had to have the baby (TJ) delivered to save both of their lives. Her blood pressure was 200/150 when they took her into surgery.

'My doctor missed my pre-eclampsia. If my husband wouldn't have been home that morning when I seized, and if he had not known what to do, neither I nor my baby would be here today. My son's birth weight was only 2 pounds 4 ounces, and he was only 14 inches long. He was life-flighted to Children's Memorial Hermann later that day and was in the NICU for three and a half months,' said Hancock.

Hancock didn't get to meet TJ until a week after he was born or hold him until two weeks later because she was in such bad shape. TJ has had two surgeries – both related to prematurity – and he continues to need specialist doctors, medicines, and care. There is no way to know what problems he may have in the future.

She remembers the first time she saw TJ – nothing could have prepared her for what she found in the incubator. She cried the entire drive home. 'I was eager to breastfeed my son, but couldn't due to his special needs in the hospital. I instead pumped eight times a day for four months to provide his meals – there was little else I could do for him other than that and just be at the hospital to comfort him,' said Hancock.

Of the 107 days TJ was at the hospital, they drove 90 minutes round trip – sometimes up to 3 hours with traffic – all but 4 of those days. Hancock had to return to work early and struggled to balance the care of her son with working full-time. And, when TJ came home, he had special feeding requirements due to aspiration from prematurity, severe reflux, and received the expensive Synigis shots monthly.

For the first year of TJ's life, the Hancocks lived with the constant worry of him getting ill and kept him quarantined for the most part. 'We had a sitter at our home, for the first three months after I returned to work, to keep him away from other kids. When my son turned 1 year old, he had never been to a grocery store, restaurant, or public place, other than a doctor's office,' admitted Hancock.

While in the hospital, Hancock did her best to be strong, pushing down the emotions and fear just to concentrate on squeezing in every moment she could to be there for TJ. She did as much as she could, as far as care for him, while there – changing diapers, taking temperature, running errands for the nurse staff, staying on top of his medical records, pumping milk, reading or singing to him in his incubator, and holding him (kangaroo style) as much as she could.

Even though Hancock had a great family support system in place, she didn't use it. She felt compelled to be strong and fearless on the outside so that everyone else would worry less or she feared losing what little control she had. She felt that she was failing her son if she wasn't there at the hospital every day.

Leaving her job wasn't an option because he was insured under Hancock's benefits. 'We racked up $800,000 in medical bills in the first nine months of his life, and we didn't know what the future would hold. My workplace gave me a lot of flexibility. I took the first six weeks of disability to recover, and then I worked from home, the office and the hospital, depending on my needs. I then was able to take an additional six weeks of disability to care for my son when he came home from the hospital,' said Hancock.

Once TJ came home from the hospital, the extra flexibility her employer offered with the doctor appointments, surgeries, and extra care he needed was key. Now that TJ is 18 months, things have started to slow down, and they are starting to try for a second child. They moved insurance over to her husband's employer, in case they are faced with the same situation again.

Hancock admitted she was nervous that she would be let go. 'My office had just gone through a number of cuts before my son was born. I was nervous about two-plus months of my home-hospital-office working model and then another six weeks off. Even when I came back, I was not as focused as I was before. My husband is a contract worker, so we were very worried about him taking time off or away from the office,' she said. 'With all the medical bills and insurance needs, it was a very stressful time from many angles. Overall, my boss was extremely supportive, as were my teams, and I couldn't have gotten through it without them. My teams really stepped up and took a lot of work off my plate so I could be at the hospital as much as I could.'

Hancock took conference calls from the NICU lounge and learned to cradle TJ while typing on her laptop in his NICU pod. It was a rough balance that continued when he came home and had a lot of special care needs and doctor appointments. Balancing work and a premature infant was challenging for Hancock, but with a supportive work environment, husband and family, they made it work.

Managing a Sick Child

Based on expert advice, here are tips for caring for a sick baby:

- Plan ahead. 'Make sure to set personal days aside to stay home with the inevitable sick child. A baby or toddler in daycare will almost certainly come home with a cold or ear infection a couple of times each flu season. And school-age children are notorious for passing germs back and forth,' said Gilman. Caudle advised moms to come up with plan B now – don't wait until the morning someone wakes up with a fever or has vomited all night.
- Talk to your boss in advance about office policies for sick

children. 'This may be especially important if you don't receive paid time off or have to find someone to replace your shift. Bringing it up ahead of time helps you anticipate if you'll have the ability to flex your schedule to accommodate illness. Being able to work from home while your child is sick could be a large advantage,' said Gilman.

- Work with your employer to determine what options are available *beforehand*. Caudle's employer has a 'sick daycare' option available. 'However, the kids need to be registered with shot records on file before you can take advantage. Check into those things, and if you think you may need to use something like that, get the requirements taken care of and keep records up to date so you aren't trying to get those things together with a sick child in tow,' she advised.

- If you can, stay home from work. 'Some employers allow their workers to use sick days to care for children. Others allow folks to work from home when their children are ill, or allow workers to bring their sick children to work with them. If you stay home, there are many options available to keep you tied in, such as conference calls or video links for attending meetings,' said Caudle.

- Employ help from others. Gilman said to think about trading off mornings or afternoons with your spouse or partner – each of you can try to be in the office for the most critical periods of the day, get your work done, then leave to trade off with your spouse. Don't think you have to do it alone because you are the mom; if your husband has the ability to split the time, then utilize this resource. Set up a system with other available caregivers to be 'on call' when baby gets sick – perhaps grandparents, aunts or uncles, neighbors – those who could help out in a pinch and allow some time for you to get work done at the office if required.

Establishing a Nursing Schedule

I was fortunate to be able to nurse both my daughters and work around their feeding schedules. I breastfed Kaitlyn for 14 months (I was pregnant with Emma when I stopped) and Emma for nine months. I felt relieved I did not have to commute into an office daily since I was nursing throughout the night when my girls were babies and would often be fatigued during the day, due to lack of sleep.

My work-from-home strategy was to set important calls during their scheduled nap times. It was tricky at times – I remember a situation in which I had to step out of a call because Kaitlyn would not stop crying in her crib. On certain days, I brought in a babysitter when I needed to be at the computer for a five-hour assignment. I made sure I had enough milk pumped for that block of time.

Lindsay Olson, partner and recruiter at Paradigm Staffing and co-founder of Hoojobs.com, told me her biggest challenge in raising a baby to toddler while working was managing the feeding issue. 'My child would never take a bottle, so I quickly gave up on the idea of pumping and figured out a way to make it work. We nursed exclusively until she turned 2, and she self-weaned. Especially in the first year or so, it was difficult, and I made some sacrifices to be as close as possible and make it work,' said Olson.

Olson took the first four months off to be with her baby, but shortly after, she needed to get back to the office. Olson physically moved her office just a few blocks from her home, so she could easily get back home to nurse every two to three hours and then get back to the office without being out for very long, or her nanny could bring her daughter to the office to nurse before going out for errands.

'While running back and forth during the day wasn't comfortable for two years, I'm so glad I was able to work it out and come up with a solution to be able to give my child what she needed and have that connection throughout the day during a time that was so important for her development,' admitted Olson.

Olson always intended to breastfeed, but she never realized that babies sometimes reject the bottle, like hers did. Olson and her husband had to attend a weeklong work conference when her baby was five months old. It meant traveling internationally. They thought before becoming parents that Olson would be able to pump and leave enough milk for a five-month-old and that her baby would stay contently with her grandparents for that week. So they booked tickets, paid for the hotel, and set up lots of meetings.

'I realized that leaving our five-month-old with the grandparents and with pumped milk would be impossible in our situation. Not only would she not take a bottle but also the amount of preparation and time to make that much breast milk available for her during that time away would have been a serious undertaking,' said Olson. 'We had already invested a lot of time and money into the event and couldn't cancel it, so I arranged to bring my mother-in-law with us to the event (from Argentina!) to stay with my daughter. We arranged accommodation in the hotel right next to the convention center, so she could call me every two hours when my daughter needed me, and I would come back to nurse her, or she would bring her to me at the convention center. We did this for a week, the four of us sharing a hotel room, and it worked fabulously!'

Olson never tired of breastfeeding during those two years. Yes, physically, she was tired. The baby never slept through the night once (or went to bed without Olson) until two weeks before her second birthday. 'She always woke up to nurse at least once in the night. It got easier as she got older actually. She needed me much less. The trips home in the middle of the day started to lessen after the first year. She could get through much longer time periods without needing me,' said Olson.

The economy definitely affected their situation, but not Olson's decision to nurse. 'I'm self-employed, a recruiter, so when hiring is down, my work is definitely down. The economy didn't force me to decide to work or be a stay-at-home mom, though,' she said. 'I've always known I would work and raise my children. My industry started to pop back up right when I came back from maternity leave, so it wasn't as bad as it was during my pregnancy with my daughter.'

Two experts offer advice on how best to manage the infant feeding schedule. About the time many mothers return to work after maternity leave (12 weeks), babies are eating about every three to four hours, so if you are working and breastfeeding you should try to pump milk every three hours. 'If using formula, babies tend to fill up for slightly longer periods of time, so feeding may be closer to every four hours at this time. They are eating about six to eight times per day. At this point, babies may be able to sleep longer periods in the night because they are more active and alert during the day. You may be able to have six to eight hours at night without feedings,' said Gilman.

After four months, babies are eating on demand, and rice cereal and solid foods are added to the baby's schedule so it gets easer – feedings may begin to dwindle, but Gilman said you still have to find time to pump if you're breastfeeding. Babies are continuing to sleep long stretches at night.

Gilman has helped a number of clients establish good sleep hygiene to reinforce this natural milestone that babies are reaching. Her quick sleep tips:

- Learn the baby's signals that he is tired, such as rubbing eyes or nose, pulling at ears, being more fussy than usual, and put the baby in the crib when you begin to see him exhibiting this behavior to reinforce putting baby down *before* he falls asleep so he goes to bed sleepy but still awake.

- Teach your baby the difference between night and day by interacting with her frequently and keeping the house bright and not worrying about normal daytime noise. If baby wakes during the night, keep lights low and noise at a minimum – no playing or too much stimulation at night wakings.
- Begin a simple bedtime routine about 15 minutes prior to the time baby usually falls asleep. For example, bathing or washing down, changing into pajamas, and reading a book or singing a song before putting baby in the crib.

Employed mothers' infant feeding practices may be shaped by time constraints and convenience. 'Many mothers choose to stop breastfeeding and switch to formula after maternity leave because they don't have time to pump at work, or don't have privacy to pump. This can be very stressful and disappointing for many mothers who feel they are forced to give up something they feel is important to their child's healthy development,' added Gilman. 'I have worked with several mothers who experienced a tremendous amount of guilt because they had to stop breastfeeding.'

'We all know that breast milk is best for our babies (not to mention free) and more and more, I believe women are aspiring at least to some period of exclusive nursing for their babies. Getting off to a good start is essential,' said Caudle.

Here are Caudle's pointers:

- Have a lactation consultant lined up before birth. If needed, work with that person before you return to work. Unless you can nurse while at work, you'll need to pump.
- Once you are sure you can nurse successfully, buy (or better yet, rent) two breast pumps. Get good ones. And buy extra storage bottles for when you are just too tired to clean them at night.

- Leave one pump at work and use the other one at home when needed to keep your supply up. Before you go on maternity leave, make sure there will be a place for you to pump. Familiarize yourself thoroughly with your pump, where you'll clean the parts in between uses, and where you'll store the milk until you take it home.

Some women simply cannot nurse their babies adequately. 'It's not a sign of failure. It's just how it is. If you feel your baby isn't getting enough from you, talk to the pediatrician or your lactation consultant,' said Caudle. 'Maintaining supply once back at work has been a significant challenge for me and many friends. If you have to supplement with formula, then you are not a failure. You are actually in quite good company, and all our babies have grown up to be geniuses.'

Toddler Tantrum Issues

As I mentioned, Kaitlyn (almost 4 years old), like some of her friends and classmates, is prone to meltdowns when she does not get her way. Jason and I don't want to raise a spoiled brat so we are working on taming these tantrums. Perhaps we have been too indulgent and given in at times when we shouldn't have.

I have been in public situations with Kaitlyn where she has been in hysteria, kicking and screaming. Some incidents have been related to her fatigue; others, because she did not get what she wanted. My solution is to remove her from the scene as calmly as possible and put her in a time-out when she is home.

Tantrums are a result of giving into children, and children learn that they can get their way by acting in a dramatic way. 'The child has learned to tantrum from conditioning, not logic or reason. Consequences of getting his or her way shape behavior. When a child uses a tantrum to get his or her own way, the parent needs to immediately remove the child to a time-out area,' Gilman said. 'This is done unemotionally, but with a firm voice –

no anger or apology of any kind. The parent simply must say, "When you behave this way, you may not be with us." And remove the child to a time-out location. This has to be done immediately and every single time the child tantrums. This also has to be done the same way each time, so the child learns exactly what to expect.'

How should time-outs be implemented? 'Time-out is extremely effective – but should only be used between the ages of 2 and 12 years. The child should understand the time-out procedure. Time-out should be applied immediately after bad behavior occurs. Pick a boring place for time-out with no stimuli,' she said. 'Place your child in time-out using no more than ten words and within ten seconds of behavior occurring. Label the behavior that got the child sent to time-out; for example, "Hitting your sister is against the rules." Set a portable timer to ring after two minutes. Tell the child when he or she hears the timer that the child can get up but not until that time. Give the child no attention while in time-out. After the timer rings, process with your child what behavior sent him or her to time-out.'

Little offered this advice for managing these toddler tantrums: 'Mothers need to be on the same page as their childcare providers. This means they need to be consistent in how they manage behaviors as well as recognize what behaviors are age-appropriate and typical (for example, the 18- to 30-month-old "no" for everything), including what they want.'

Discuss with your childcare provider what they find challenging and how they manage those behaviors. 'Consistency of techniques and consequences are the key to management. Just because the toddler throws a fit at being left with the provider, it doesn't mean that the parent should be guilt-ridden because the child is upset,' she said. 'Most likely, the child is suddenly experiencing the awareness of being separated from the parent (typical of the age), and the parent should ignore the behaviors.

Guaranteed, the provider ignores these, and very quickly the child is off to the adventures of the day.'

'Screaming children in the grocery store on the way home from work may be an embarrassment or an annoyance, but children act that way because parents reinforce the behavior in some way (giving in to a candy bar, holding them, promising extra treats when they get home),' said Little. 'Again, the consistency is important. Of course, children always seem to act up when parents are stressed about something (such as time, telephone calls, guests arriving, and so forth). When the parent yells, screams, shouts, or hits, the child wins, and the behavior will escalate.'

The best approach, said Little, is to speak quietly and calmly while making close eye contact with the child. The child wants the parent's attention and that is the best way to give it (calmly, quietly, and in control).

The primary goal of 2- and 3-year-olds is to establish their independence and enforce their will. 'They just realized they aren't directly connected to their mommy and actually have minds of their own. Unfortunately, they don't have the cognitive skills or emotional control to go along with their very strong wills,' said Caudle. 'That means that we, as parents, can't allow them to do everything they want to. This is a recipe for... tantrums.'

Her advice as a mother? 'When it counts, hold your ground. If you're exhausted, and you still have to make dinner, pack lunches, do homework, and vacuum, don't set a limit on your toddler when you don't have the energy or time to enforce it,' she said. 'Some fights just aren't worth fighting. Sometimes cereal is an adequate dinner. Sometimes you can "change your mind" without losing complete control of your little monster.'

When I see Kaitlyn being good (sharing toys, cleaning up her room), I try to reinforce these behaviors on a regular basis by praising her. Gilman told me this is wise, and good behavior should be rewarded quickly and often. 'Social rewards are very effective with kids to strengthen good behavior. Smiles, pats, hugs, kisses, words of praise – these help teach kids what is expected of them,' she said. 'Be specific: "I like the way you're sharing your blocks with Susie – it makes me proud," or "Your room looks good – you did such a great job cleaning up the toys." If you don't tell your kids you appreciate or like things they do, they will stop doing them.'

Material and activity rewards are also effective – a small toy, extra computer or iPad time, special dessert, going to the park, having a friend over,' said Gilman. 'To be effective, rewards must be immediate.'

Be careful not to accidentally reward or pay attention to undesirable or even bad behavior. 'Parents sometimes give in because they are tired of listening to whining or complaining, so to get the child to stop, they agree to the child's request. If you give in, then you unintentionally reinforce the whining and complaining; these behaviors are more likely to increase in the future,' added Gilman. How to deal with 'pre-tantrum' – whining, whimpering, begging – behavior: 'When this behavior occurs, never ever give in or reinforce the behavior. Say to your child in a calm, unemotional voice: "You may not have that" or "Talk to me with your best voice." If the whining persists, say: "When you behave this way you cannot be with me," and lead your child to a designated time-out area. In a store, remove the child to a quiet, solitary area and turn your attention away from him or her until the behavior stops. If it persists, then leave and do normal time-out at home.'

Chapter 8

Childcare: What's the Best Solution?

Quality childcare is critical for infants and toddlers. Many mothers struggle with returning to work full-time after maternity leave. They feel guilty being away from their babies and miss them throughout the day. For the majority of working families today, both spouses (or partners) have to work. Or one spouse is working while the other is unemployed due to the economic downturn. It's no longer the generation of the stay-at-home mom who tends to house and kids while Dad is the sole breadwinner.

Our childcare situation was not traditional. For the first year-and-one-half of my daughters' lives, I worked when they napped during the day and were asleep at night. When she was 18 months old, we put Kaitlyn in Moonstone Preschool for three days a week. Same with Emma – we put her in Moonstone at the same age for three days a week. I get a babysitter as needed when they are not in school and continue to work early morning or evenings to meet deadlines.

I did local research on daycares before Kaitlyn was born. I asked mom friends and city moms at the park (or play dates) what they were doing and which centers were the most reputable. When Kaitlyn was just a few months old, I toured several daycares that were within walking distance and highly regarded. I knew there were waiting lists at the city daycares, so I did not procrastinate and put Kaitlyn on these lists. We were thrilled to get notification she was accepted into Moonstone. It was the perfect start for her early childhood development.

Wise moms seek out the opinions and recommendations of other mothers, if possible, agreed Marissa Kiepert Truong, PhD, an educational psychologist in Philadelphia and former director at Kindercare. In addition to the local library or playground, 'community pages on Facebook or other online networks are also great places to connect with other working mothers,' she said. A mother can 'check the availability of the different childcare options in her area via the Internet. A quick search should return daycares or nanny placement agencies. See what mothers are saying online. A search for rankings, ratings, and reviews of the type of childcare a mother has chosen can be quite telling.'

Kiepert Truong offered other pointers:

- Conduct a face-to-face meeting.
- If you are interested in daycares, visit several for a tour. Be prepared to ask many questions regarding the health, safety, and education provided.
- If looking for a nanny, you should conduct multiple interviews.
- Ask for references. Once you have narrowed down your search to a few options, ask for references of the child's new teacher or nanny.

Determine Individual Needs

'Every individual has a different childcare selection process. To find the best childcare for your children, self-reflect, educate yourself on the options available, and conduct research to assure yourself that the chosen care is of the utmost quality,' said Kiepert Truong.

First take some time to think about your needs are and what options work well for *your* family. To begin, Kiepert Truong said you might want to consider asking yourself:

- What are the childcare options that are accessible to me?
- What hours of the day do I need someone to care for my child?
- How many hours a day will I need childcare?
- Do I need consistency or flexibility in a childcare provider?

- What is my budget for childcare?
- What do I want my *child* to get out of childcare?

Answers to these questions will determine the course of action taken into finding the best care. For example, Kiepert Truong said if you have a position where you are not working standard daytime hours, a daycare might not be the best option; few are open in the evenings. In contrast, if you cannot miss work at the last minute, then the dependability of daycare might be a good option, as a nanny who becomes ill would leave you without care for the day.

'Mothers must first decide what is important to them and their unique temperament and age of their child. I would encourage mothers to tour and interview childcare centers to see firsthand the environment and if there is a rapport with the staff. There is no substitute for a firsthand account,' said Stephanie Somanchi, MBA, PhD, an executive life coach based in Portland, Oregon.

Location, curriculum, access in the day to the child, and child-to-caregiver ratios are common concerns, said Somanchi.

Brenda Zofrea, a child safety advocate and author of *Let's B Safe* (Createspace, 2004), said obviously the center must be safe, clean, caring, and affordable. She agreed that one way parents could find the best childcare for their children is by choosing one that comes with recommendations from other parents whom you trust or have parenting values that align with yours. Remember that a 'perfect' place probably doesn't exist. Your child's safety and well-being must always come first.

Zofrea suggested you consider these questions:

- As you visit various childcare centers, pay attention to your gut instinct. How do you feel when you walk in the door? Chances are your child will feel the same way. Does it 'feel' safe, warm, welcoming, and nurturing? Never dismiss or overlook the power of your own internal instinct or 'warning system.'

- Does the center have an open door policy? Are you welcome to visit anytime during the day unannounced? If not, then Zofrea would look elsewhere.
- Is their staffing reliable and consistent? High turnover, which is very common at childcare centers, will not provide the most consistent, stable care for your child.
- Does the center have a low child-to-staff ratio? Do they have enough staff on hand to adequately care for the children enrolled at their center?
- Are all staff members trained in CPR and first aid?

Zofrea would choose a childcare center that not only has a policy that includes background checks on their employees but also one that includes both mandatory, research-based training on the prevention of sexual abuse for their employees, staff, and parents, and prevention education in their curriculum for the children in their care. 'This sends a loud message to any interested employees or volunteers that center staff is vigilant about protecting children while also providing children with the knowledge they need to help keep themselves safe,' she said.

Various Options Are Available

Amanda Armstrong, mother of two children, and president and founder of Sitter Pals, a social network for parents and trusted sitters, has investigated in-home daycare to full-time daycare centers and even regular babysitters. She even explored several options for her children to provide the best solution depending on the situation. When Armstrong returned to work full-time, she hired a regular babysitter to care for her daughter Elsie part-time. The remainder of the workweek, her husband worked from home and took care of Elsie until she was over a year old. As a premature baby, they were advised by their pediatrician to keep Elsie out of daycare for at least the first year.

As a result, Elsie remained healthy and their part-time arrangement with their babysitter worked well. At 14 months, they found a full-time daycare center to provide more flexibility and freedom for their work schedules. 'The financial investment was equivalent to the most expensive private high school in our area, something that came as a total shock to a first-time mother. For various reasons, we decided to move Elsie from the daycare center to an in-home daycare, as referred to us by family and friends,' said Armstrong.

The in-home daycare provided a small trusted group of children, a provider with an excellent record, and a more cost-effective alternative to a full-time daycare facility. 'When I was pregnant with my second child and placed on bed rest after going into preterm labor at 29 weeks, we sought babysitters through my network of friends to help with my 2-year-old daughter,' said Armstrong. 'Having Elsie home with me was also important to keep both of us healthy, as illness and dehydration were triggers for my preterm labor. Today Elsie is in preschool three days a week and my 1-year-old son is in preschool two days a week, along with a regular sitter one day a week.'

Armstrong said that moms need to listen to their intuition, as well as do the research on facilities and providers to make sure they are placing their child in a clean and safe environment. 'Ask about their teacher-to-child ratios and other policies, such as biting, sick children, how they handle discipline with children and how they notify parents. If you are hiring a babysitter or nanny, ask how they handle disciplining the children and their philosophies on child development. Set the expectations and keep the lines of communication open as much as possible with your provider,' she said.

In addition, network with mothers of children the same age or older than yours to find trusted babysitters and nannies. 'Other mothers are the first to know when a great nanny or babysitter is available for a new family. Talk with other moms about their experiences with childcare to understand variables you would not have anticipated, such as jealousy and guilt,' added Armstrong.

Paid Parental Leave Is Vital

Sadly, only about half of all first-time moms in the US are able to take a paid leave after childbirth, and just a fifth of working mothers receive leave with full pay, according to the most recent census data by the advocacy group National Partnership for Women and Families. A Families and Work Institute report found that only 16 percent of the companies it surveyed offered full paid maternity leave in 2008, down from 27 percent in 1998.

Working Mother magazine launched an ambitious four-year campaign to change this. Their goal is to ensure paid parental leave is available to all US workers by 2015, their thirtieth anniversary year.

The Family and Medical Leave Act (FMLA) mandates 12 weeks of leave (job-guaranteed) for caregivers. FMLA is unpaid, so many parents cannot afford to take this time off.

Childcare Costs Are Increasing

Many working mothers are faced with other tough choices since the childcare expense is increasing despite the weakened economy. Childcare is simply not affordable for many working families dealing with lengthy unemployment, reduced salaries and no healthcare benefits.

According to a report released in August 2011 by the National Association of Childcare Resource and Referral Agencies (NACCRRA), the cost of childcare continues to increase while families struggle to afford quality care. *Parents and the High Cost of Childcare: 2011 Update* provides results from a survey of Childcare Resource and Referral (CCR&R) state networks and local agencies, which asked for the average fees charged by childcare programs in 2010.

The report, which provides the average cost of childcare for infants, 4-year-olds, and school-age children in centers and family childcare homes nationwide, revealed that in 36 states, the average annual cost for center-based care for an infant was higher than a year's tuition and related fees at a four-year public college. In every state, center-based childcare costs for two children (an infant and a 4-year-old) exceeded annual average rent payments.

'Childcare is essential to working families, and working families are key to economic growth,' said Linda K. Smith, NACCRRA's executive director. 'But childcare today is simply unaffordable for most families.'

According to the report, in 2010, the average annual cost of full-time care for an infant in a center ranged from $4,650 in Mississippi to $18,200 in the District of Columbia. Parents of a 4-year-old child paid average fees of $3,900 in Mississippi to $14,050 per year in the District of Columbia. In New York, parents of school-age children paid up to $10,400 a year for part-time care in a center. The report also found that in 2010, the average annual cost of full-time care in a family childcare home was as much as $12,100 for an infant and $11,300 for a 4-year-old in Massachusetts.

'During the critical years of birth through age 5, 90 percent of a child's brain is developed and essential learning patterns are established which affect school-readiness,' said Smith. 'Children need to be safe in childcare, and they also need to be in a setting that promotes their healthy development or our early childhood policies undermine our school readiness goals. It is time for policymakers to recognize that connection. Children spend an average of 35 hours a week in childcare which means childcare is a key early learning program.'

In the United States, more than 11 million children under age 5 are in childcare each week and although childcare costs are high, most states have inadequate requirements for the quality of care. Currently, the federal Childcare and Development Block

Grant (CCDBG), which provides funds to states to help make childcare more affordable for families, does not require that funds be used to pay for licensed care. Nationally, more than 20 percent of children who receive CCDBG assistance are in unlicensed settings. In nine states, 35 percent or more of the children who receive this assistance are in unlicensed settings.

Unlicensed settings do not have to meet state health or safety standards, providers are not required to be trained, and the settings are not inspected. 'No one knows about the quality of care offered in unlicensed settings, which means children are really left to chance,' said Smith. 'There should be more accountability for quality when government funds are used to pay for childcare,' Smith said.

Lower Cost Alternatives

What are some alternative lower-cost solutions to childcare centers?

'Sharing a nanny or babysitter with a close friend can help cut down on cost, while also bringing in more social interaction with other children. Find families with similar needs and values through your place of employment or network of friends,' advised Armstrong. 'Search for referrals from friends and family for in-home daycare providers, which are usually more cost-effective and which offer a smaller group of children than outside-of-the-home daycare facilities. Often, moms wanting to stay home and earn an income open their home to other children.' (This is also known as 'family daycare.')

Consider a family member to supplement care or provide full-time care if you believe the right arrangement could be made. 'When relying on family for childcare, it is important to establish a mutually agreed-upon contract, setting the rules, hours, and cost (if applicable),' added Armstrong. 'Preschools and Mother's Day Out programs are affordable part-time options for childcare, also offering curriculums and licensed or degreed early childhood education providers. Explore combining a few of these options to keep costs down, while providing enriched childcare for your child.'

Co-op childcare often offers a lower cost option in exchange for volunteer work, noted Somanchi. 'This can also offer a higher level of familiarity with the teachers and curriculum. This structure may also be more responsive to parents' needs and concerns,' she said.

Public school pre-K programs are available throughout the US. These usually run for ages 3 to 5, before kindergarten. Do research and determine if there any public school options in your area. In Philadelphia, being accepted into the city's pre-K program requires getting through its lottery system.

Center Examination

Jennifer Pereyra, a mompreneur and author of a children's book, *Mommy and Daddy Work to Make Some Dough* (Tate Publishing, 2011), evaluated the possibility of a nanny as well as an in-home daycare. 'Nannies, while offering more flexibility, tend to be a more expensive option, and we didn't feel comfortable with our baby being in an in-home daycare where she would be inter-mingled with kids of all ages,' said Pereyra.

As a result, Pereyra decided to go with center-based childcare. 'It was an interesting adventure. New mothers are decidedly imperfect in that we all believe our babies are perfect and that we will never, ever let them suck on the germ-laden car keys to keep them busy in the supermarket... or that we'll never, ever give in to temper tantrums,' she said. 'I was no different. I had my perfect beautiful baby girl that was dressed in her pink ruffles and ribbons, and was taking her with me as I chose the place where she would be spending a good chunk of her days going forward.'

Like all mothers, she had a naïve idea of grandmotherly caregivers playing with clean, cheerful babies as they rocked them back and forth. In stark contrast, Pereyra walked into one place where the babies' shirts were soaked with drool, formula, and Cheerios that had been mashed all together to make a filthy mess. Another place exuded the stench of dirty diapers from the moment she opened the front door. So as not to be rude, however, Pereyra suffered through the tour anyway as the center director talked about the usual stuff like state certification, ratios, and nap times.

In the end, Pereyra decided on a corporate-run daycare center where Rebeca started when she was just seven weeks old. Her daughter Sofia also started, and continues to attend a center-based preschool. (Her husband was a participant in the decision-making process, yet this decision tends to be one decision, fairly or not, that moms pretty much control or provide the lead on.)

It's easy to eliminate the horrific centers like the ones Pereyra mentioned above, but once you're down to two, potentially three good ones, how do you really differentiate between them? 'Well, since our family has relocated twice for career advancement opportunities, I know a thing or two about evaluating center-based daycare and preschool,' said Pereyra. 'There are two key questions that I have found help to distinguish between good centers and great centers: "How long has each of your head classroom teachers been employed here?" and "Tell me about your teaching philosophy – what is the preschool curriculum like?"'

The first question is regarding the tenure of the head teachers of each of the classrooms; you're not looking for the numbers of years of total experience, but rather, how long they have been at that particular center. 'This is important because daycare centers and preschools have some of the highest rates of turnover of any industry (between 25 and 40 percent),' said Pereyra. Prior to finding the center Sofia currently attends and from which Rebeca graduated pre-K, Pereyra had come to accept the constantly changing faces as the norm. Sofia's current center has been open since the year 2000, and all but two or three of their head teachers have been there since the day they opened their doors.

In addition to a particularly high retention rate, Pereyra also began to notice other things that were different from their previous experiences. The rooms were always overstaffed, so there was never a concern that the child-to-teacher ratio was going to fall below what was required. In the director's office, there are monitors with both video and audio from which she regularly observes the teachers and assistants. In addition, there are continual improvements being made to the facility like fresh paint, new carpets, and so forth.

Pereyra's personal conclusion is that the owners (it's a national franchise) are on-site regularly. They manage the place properly in every aspect of the business from customer service, to facility maintenance, to employee retention. Because customer service and facility maintenance aren't necessarily things that are tracked regularly or that could be compared from center to center, the only hard number one could ask for would be their head teacher retention rate. Pereyra believes that retention rate is one way to distinguish good centers from great ones.

The next question came about because of a lack of foresight on Pereyra's part. Pereyra had hoped that, once they knew where they were going to live, they would find a center, and Rebeca would be able to stay in that same center until she started kindergarten. 'Overall we were pleased with the center we had found. However, after being there for some time we began to notice that the only projects she was bringing home were art projects. At that point, she was 3 years old, and I was expecting that they would have started to write letters and numbers,' she said.

After some time had passed, Pereyra approached the center director to inquire as to when they would start more structured learning. She explained that their teaching philosophy was one of strictly learning through play. They didn't believe in providing a structured curriculum until the child reaches kindergarten.

The Pereyras ended up changing centers because they felt that Rebeca, while strong artistically, would benefit from a more structured learning environment. Had they asked that question up front, then they never would have enrolled Rebeca in that center in the first place.

Daycare vs. Nanny

Some working moms I know have chosen to go with nannies when their kids were babies, but then move them into daycare centers when they were at least a year old – when toddlers have stronger immune systems and seek more interaction with others their age. Which is better for your baby or toddler – state-licensed daycare or an in-home nanny? Kiepert Truong offered a summary of pros and cons of these two popular childcare options:

Daycare: Pros

- Standardized policies and procedures help to ensure the health and safety of children
- Centers generally conduct background checks, such as criminal and child abuse, on staff and teachers
- A child learns socialization skills through interaction with others; cognitive skills are also enhanced through daily lessons
- Care will always be available, provided the daycare is not closed for a holiday or professional development day
- An age-appropriate curriculum is provided for children
- Centers provide developmental or educational progress reports, formally or informally

Daycare: Cons

- Some centers may be inflexible with hours and days of care

- Due to close interaction with other children, a child can be put at greater risk of catching colds or other contagious illnesses
- There is less flexibility and individuality in a child's schedule, as all students follow the same routine
- A child receives less individualized attention because teachers or caregivers are looking after several children at once
- Daycares are often closed on most major holidays
- Families are often only given a week or two of 'vacation' time a year, and are expected to pay tuition rates regardless of whether the child attends

Nanny: Pros

- A child is given the nanny's full attention
- There is more flexibility in scheduling; a nanny may work mornings one day and evenings the next
- A child is able to stay in the comfort of his or her own home
- Mothers can set a pay rate for the nanny that they feel comfortable with
- The child's schedule is built around the mother's desires
- A child isn't confined to one space all day and has the freedom to visit parks, museums, libraries, and so forth

Nanny: Cons

- It may be difficult to trust someone 'unknown'
- Nannies can call off work or quit unexpectedly, leaving mothers with no childcare
- There is no set learning curriculum being followed
- There may not be checks and balances on the care the nanny is providing

If you decide a nanny will be best for your childcare needs, take your time and do not rush to a decision. Interview many candidates. Discuss with your spouse or partner the type of person who is best suited to care for your baby. Do not hire someone until you are certain she will be the best fit. You are essentially hiring an employee, and this is not a decision to be taken lightly.

Guidelines to Hire a Nanny

Candi Wingate, president of Nannies4Hire, a company that specializes in finding high caliber, experienced nannies and au pairs for families across the United States and Canada, offered some tips on finding the best nanny for your family:

1 Determine what you want in a nanny. What skills do you want your nanny to possess? Do you want a nanny to perform other tasks? (For example, do you want her to do your children's laundry?)

2 Write a job description and draft a nanny contract. You can find template forms for both of these documents online.

3 Search a database of available nannies online. You can search a database by your locale, and screen nannies based on the skills you are looking for.

4 When you have identified several nannies who may be a good fit for your family, call or email those nannies to set a time for a telephone interview with them.

5 By telephone, give a brief interview to each nanny candidate who meets your baseline qualifications. Ask basic, job-related questions, such as, 'What do you like about being a nanny?' or 'Please tell me about your most difficult experience as a nanny and how you handled it.'

6 For each nanny candidate who met your expectations, schedule an in-person interview to be held in a neutral location such as a coffee shop. These 'screening' interviews should not involve your children. During these interviews,

ask your nanny candidates more in-depth, job-related questions, such as, 'Have you ever been convicted of a felony or any potentially job-related misdemeanor?' or 'What hours are you available to work?'. Provide each nanny candidate with a copy of the job description and respond to any questions she may have about its contents; and have her sign authorizations for you to perform background checks.

7 Perform background checks.

8 For each nanny candidate who met your expectations through step 7, set an in-person interview to be held in your home. These selection interviews should include your children so that you can observe how each nanny candidate relates with your children. If old enough, your children may also form an opinion about which nanny candidate they prefer. The wise mom considers her child's perspectives, but does not feel required to hire whomever the child prefers. As the parent, you need to hire based on your wisdom and parental perspective.

9 Once your family has decided which nanny is the best candidate, it is time to offer your nanny position to your best candidate. The initial job offer should occur by telephone.

10 During the job offer discussion, negotiate compensation, benefits, start date, and other terms and conditions of employment.

11 Update your nanny contract with information.

12 Send a formal job offer letter to your best candidate. Enclose in the envelope a copy of the updated nanny contract, the job description, a W-4 form (for payroll purposes), an I-9 form (for documentation of identity and eligibility to work in the United States), and any other employment-related document that is necessary in your area.

13 Have your new nanny sign and date the job description and nanny contract on or before her first day of employment with you. On her first day of employment, ensure that she completes the W-4 and Section 1 of the I-9 form. Within the first three business days of her employment, you will need to complete the employer portion of the I-9 form as well. If your area requires other employment-related documents at the time of hire, those documents will need to be completed promptly also.

Chapter 9

Support: Who's My Care Network?

Working mothers may feel isolated post-birth, especially if they don't have friends and family close by to help them out. New moms need all the support they can get while caring for babies, feeding on demand, and coping with their own sleep deprivation. Yet, support is also needed beyond a baby's first year.

I remember my situation – nursing every two to three hours in the first few months of my daughters' lives. It could get stressful, and I did feel isolated and house-bound at times after Kaitlyn was born. We don't have family in the immediate area, and, while I have many casual friends, few seemed close enough to call on in the event of an emergency. My mother would tell me she wished she lived closer to us so she could lend a hand throughout the week.

With my first newborn, I attended a breastfeeding group at Pennsylvania Hospital several times. I enjoyed meeting other new moms and hearing their newborn stories and concerns. There I met a woman I am friends with today – and she informed me about the Moms Club of Philadelphia.

I joined the Moms Club in January 2009 at her recommendation. I was looking to meet other mothers for lunch or breaks and talk about our kids' development. The Moms Club (http://www.momsclub.org) has chapters across the country. They are a support group for stay-at-home and working mothers. Each local chapter offers its own activities for moms and their children.

Our chapter has down-to-earth moms who get together when we can for activities such as coffee breaks, walks in the park, play dates at a member's house, trips to the zoo, and so forth. We also have a Mom's Night Out each month and quarterly socials to allow us time to have adult conversation without being distracted by our kids.

The club has been an important part of my life as a working mother. After I gave birth to Emma, the club delivered about two weeks' worth of meals so we did not have to cook during this hectic time. I have formed friendships with some club members. If ever an emergency occurred, I am certain a mom from the club would be able to help us out.

I now serve as membership VP for the Philadelphia chapter and answer questions from potential members about joining. It's a good chance for me to give back, as I've reaped benefits from being an active member of the club.

I recommend mothers look into joining their local chapter or another local moms' support group. Conduct online research to determine what your city or region has to offer – then get involved. Attend an event and see if you like the group members and if it would be a good fit. Keep searching until you find the group that will work for your schedule and needs.

Hesitant to Seek Help

Dr. Marcia Eckerd, a clinical psychologist in practice 28 years based in Norwalk, Connecticut, said in her experience, many mothers are willing to make acquaintances, but can be hesitant to look for support or help. 'They feel that they need to seem self-sufficient and in control, although many are like ducks: they seem to be gliding over the water and are paddling away furiously underneath. It's easy to become isolated,' she said. These women are setting themselves up for burnout.

'People with a community of support are healthier, live longer, and have less stress. A problem is that working mothers need to work at creating a support network, and anything that seems like more work can fall to the bottom of the priority list,' said Eckerd. 'It's hard to have the time and energy it takes to reach out and follow up.'

Some neighborhoods are friendly and child-centered with local parks and playgrounds; some workplaces lend themselves to connecting, with in-house childcare or resources such as exercise rooms. 'These are fortunate situations for meeting other women. Women in corporate settings and women working from home don't have such readily available support. Women moving from full-time work to part-time work can feel especially challenged, that they don't fit with stay-at-home moms or full-time working moms,' said Eckerd. 'Other mothers in similar situations are out there; those moms might need to use social networking in addition to the usual strategies.'

If potential support isn't so readily available, there are strategies. Eckerd shared a few:

- Go where other mothers with children the same age gather. Even if it's only on weekends, being a regular at a playground and attending a child's activities are good ways to meet. Mothers can 'hang out' while their children play.
- Volunteer to be on a board or committee. Some boards only meet once monthly. Over a year, members spend a substantial amount of time talking, hearing each other's ideas, and getting a sense of who appeals as a potential friend. This is a good route for part-time workers.
- A support group doesn't have to include only mothers. Doing a favorite activity in a group works to meet people, whether it's biking, yoga, or a book club. The best part is that it's time when a mom can refuel and do something for herself.

In looking for support, it's important to find people who are comfortable and don't judge. 'Competition over the "best" child or what is "best mothering" isn't support. Women need to be interested in reciprocal relationships, not a one-way chance to vent,' added Eckerd. 'The level of relationships can vary: someone who shares an interest, women sharing survival information such as good babysitters, someone who can provide emergency childcare coverage, and women who provide a deeper friendship – all of these are valuable.'

Mothers are also increasingly getting virtual support by turning to the Internet, blogs, and social networking. Eckerd mentioned sites such as http://www.workitmom.com and http://themamabee.com that share information, tweets, forums, and so forth.

Economic downturns compound the problem of finding time. 'People feel pressed to be more productive, working longer hours, and even working at home evenings and weekends. This is not only exhausting; mothers can also feel what little time is left should be spent with the children,' said Eckerd. 'It can be harder to afford babysitters or do the kinds of things that get you out of the home to meet people. It's at these times, though, that keeping in touch for support is especially important. Even a phone call or text message helps. Working mothers are "giving" all day and night; if they don't have a chance to "receive" as well, they burn out and are less available, not more, to all those other demands.'

Lacking Local Support

Camesha Gosha, creator and writer of Bibs and Baubles, is working on developing a local support system. She and her husband live in California, far from their families in Illinois and Michigan. 'For this reason, we lack a support system when it comes to our son. We are all we have for the most part. It hit us fully this year when our son came home with a note from his daycare reminding us that we hadn't listed anyone else on his forms as an approved caretaker – we'd only listed each other,' she said. 'The daycare wanted to know if there was anyone else we trusted to pick him up or care for him if we weren't available.

Our answer – no, not really.'

Gosha said they initially didn't have many friends who had children. 'So while our time became limited after having a child, theirs didn't. They've gone on to build other friendships with people who have more in common with them, and we've gone on to do the same now,' she said. 'Since we don't spend as much time with them as we used to, that makes it hard to create a support system where our son is concerned. They can't provide much support because he doesn't know them very well. We wouldn't entrust him to someone he doesn't fully trust just because we do.'

Gosha is cultivating more friendships with people who are in the same stage of life as they are. She has met people through blogs (she's a blogger), a new mom group at the hospital where their son was born, and co-workers who are embarking on the same parenthood journey.

Petra H. Maxwell, MA, JD from Harvard Law School and founder of Mediationline, understands both the challenge and importance of developing a network of people and institutions around you that you can call upon when the going gets difficult, speaking as a working mother herself, and hearing about this issue from friends, colleagues as well as clients.

This is a topic that's close to her heart because it was one of her greatest struggles when she first became a single mom about seven years ago. Maxwell had only recently moved to New York City, so she still hadn't developed many close personal friends there, had no family around for support, and was suddenly divorced with a 4-year-old child.

At that time, she was running a fairly large non-profit agency and was overwhelmed juggling the work, household, and parenting responsibilities. There were many days when she would shut her office door and have herself a good long cry.

'Most working mothers, me included, tend to be women who are resourceful, responsible, multitaskers. Therefore, when a crisis hits – such as a family illness, a job loss, or a divorce – it never even occurs to us to ask for help. We usually just hunker down and try to work harder,' said Maxwell. 'I finally reached a breaking point myself when I realized that the level of stress in my life was affecting my relationship with my child, it was affecting my work, and it was affecting my health. So, I tried to come up with a plan for how I was going to turn things around and reach out for support.'

Meetup Groups Were a Lifeline

Although Maxwell is a shy introvert by nature, she made a conscious effort to begin by asking colleagues out to lunch and dinner as a way to make new friends. She did some online research, signed up with an outfitter, and began taking active vacations by herself as a way to meet new people who enjoyed similar activities.

As she became more comfortable socially, Maxwell joined meetup groups, and they became a real lifeline for her. 'I've signed onto dating services, taken classes in the areas that I felt needed some work, gone to alumni networking events... you name it. All things I never would have had the courage to do even five years ago,' she said. 'And the effect? It's still tough to balance work and single motherhood, and I struggle to pay the bills. But I don't feel so alone anymore. In a pinch, I can call a friend when I need a shoulder to cry on, or when I want to go out for a drink, or even if I need to borrow a few bucks to get by.'

The type of support working mothers need is not just in the order of friendships. 'Working women, especially single moms, need financial support if they've come out of a marriage where their partners supported them or handled the financial affairs. Therefore, moms need to network with or develop an alliance with a trusted accountant or financial advisor who can teach them about budgeting and financial planning,' said Maxwell. 'Moms may also need help getting on track with their careers – especially if they took a break to rear children. Confronting the workforce again can be a devastating and sometimes humiliating process.'

Linking up with a good and sympathetic job coach can be a godsend for a mom who is re-entering the workforce. Maxwell works with women who are emerging from bad marriages; often such women have little or shattered self-esteem. 'Reaching out to a competent therapist – even a style consultant, dating coach, and a good hairdresser – will all help support a struggling, overworked mom as she tries to regain her feeling of self-worth and power,' she said. 'And, of course, there's absolutely no substitute for having a close friend or two on whom you can count when you need to complain or share a laugh or two over conversation. Joining groups or engaging in activities that are important to you is always the best way to meet like-minded women and men.'

For Maxwell, meetup groups that were sports related did the trick. 'Yet, joining a book club, the local church group, a political group, an exercise class, or doing volunteer work can all serve the same purpose while providing other benefits as well. If a working mom is finding herself at the point where she's feeling alone and unsupported, then she needs to make a list of the opportunities around her that make sense and that fit within her lifestyle, her budget, and her schedule,' she said. 'And then, even if it feels a bit uncomfortable at first, she needs to keep at it. It gets easier!'

Career moms need more than just friends when building a support network. The challenge of creating a good support network, Maxwell believes, starts with taking an honest look at oneself and inventorying our strengths and weaknesses as well as where we want to go with our lives. Then we need to take a hard look at the friends we currently have in our network. Are they really supporting us? Or are they holding us back? As women plan for the road ahead more thoughtfully, they may discover they need support in a variety of areas – financial planning and budgeting support with the help of a trusted accountant; career help with the support of a competent and creative coach; emotional support with the help of a great therapist; childcare assistance through the support of qualified daycare centers, babysitters, neighbors or nannies; style tips with the help of stylists, hairdressers, and aestheticians as well as personal trainers, real estate consultants, and friends,' she said. Always ask yourself: Is this person supporting the person I want to be as I move forward on my path?

The economic downturn has had a surprisingly positive effect as well. 'As hard as the recession has been for most of us, it's had a tremendous leveling effect for those of us who are in the throes of it. Now, when working moms are struggling, they can feel heartened that there are vast numbers of women – and men – out there who are undergoing similar hardships. People seem generally more sympathetic, more willing to lend a hand in any way they can because they understand the struggle now and how easy it is to be on the brink of losing everything,' Maxwell said.

Five years ago, Maxwell would have been too ashamed to admit to having financial concerns, but now she can talk about that openly, and everyone seems to be in the same boat with her. 'Many people around the country who have lost their jobs have been inspired to create something new, start their own businesses inspired by their true passions and interests. It's a crazy time, but I wouldn't say it's all bad when it comes to its effect on our interpersonal relationships,' she added.

A Business Coach Is Critical

Kelly Delaney, the owner of Cakes for Occasions, a gourmet pastry shop in the Boston area, is a nationally recognized baking expert and has grown her pastry shop into a million dollar-plus company over the past decade.

Delaney manages to juggle a young family and growing

business with the help of her husband, Frank, who is a stay-at-home dad to their young daughters who are 5 and 4. While having dad at home is the 'best case scenario' for most entrepreneurs, there are still struggles for Delaney who finds herself having to decide between that meeting with her business coach and running out to a preschool play or gym show.

'My husband is an exceptional father and caregiver, but that doesn't mean that my responsibilities to my daughters are diminished,' said Delaney. 'I still want to be a hands-on mom and that means I have to be pretty creative with how I manage my time. I have learned to be extremely efficient and to surround myself with people that can be trusted to manage things in my absence. I have also learned that a business creates some unavoidable demands; there will be some things I miss, and I had to get comfortable with that.'

Delaney said her business coach has been an invaluable support. While using a business coach does not help raise her children, it does help her manage her time more efficiently, which in turn helps her better balance being both a business owner and mother. 'Often I am pulled in multiple directions at the same time. While this can be extremely frustrating and stressful, it is my job to prioritize and recognize that something has to give. Depending on the situation, it could be a soccer game that I miss due to work,' said Delaney. 'While I try to delegate and organize work, sometimes things come up that require my attention and a game or two might be missed.'

On the flip side, there are times when Delaney is away with her family, and she either has to delegate something she would normally handle to her staff or become comfortable with the fact she cannot meet that particular deadline at that time. And many times, she learns that deadlines are not so fixed! It's amazing the power of a phone call. Sometimes just explaining the situation can yield her some flexibility that allows her to do both – see the game and get the work done.

For the first 13 years Delaney owned her business, she delivered all the wedding cakes on Sundays. She has to admit, it was a control thing for her. She needed to get out and see her customers, hear their reactions and learn as much as she could. 'During that first meeting with my coach when we went over everything, I discovered that what was a normal way of doing business for me wasn't necessarily the best use of my time. It became my coach's goal to get me to take Sundays off,' said Delaney. 'There were two reasons: one was to create a work environment that can operate without me at any time, and the second was to create additional time for me to spend with my family.'

It took Delaney close to 14 months to 'buy' into the additional expense of hiring a delivery person. After discussing the trust that is built into a position like this and how it would positively help her business, she reluctantly agreed to it. Her plan was to just use the delivery person for the summer months, but after just three weeks of having Sundays off, she is happy to report she has not delivered a cake on a Sunday in over one and a half years.

Delaney said they are lucky in that they have not been negatively affected by the economy. They have certainly tightened their belts a bit, and they do recognize that times are tough for their customers. The economy did, however, have a major impact in Delaney's work with her business coach, who had to close his business due to the poor economy. 'What I learned from him carries into my business strategy today – evaluate all the expenses that go out of my business. There is a cost or a real cost acquisition to every aspect of my business,' said Delaney. 'I also learned to recognize when it makes sense to stop doing something because it isn't yielding the results. You need to take the emotion out of the equation and look at things from a straight dollars-and-cents perspective.'

Adequate Support from Friends

Working moms cannot afford to be sick. One of my concerns has always been who would take care of the girls if I were injured or bedridden for an extended amount of time. I have drop-offs and pick-ups at two different schools during the week. I would have to find a trusted friend to shuttle them around.

Alex Hewitt, a single working mother of two boys, ages 11 and 7, faced this challenge. Hewitt lives in Baltimore and is self-employed, has a variety of jobs, and created a schedule that is flexible around the boys' school and activities schedule. Hewitt is a psychotherapist and a freelance actor of stage and screen. She teaches theater and does drama and creative therapy at a large psychiatric hospital. She also practices Bikram yoga five to seven times per week. Her boys participate in sports teams, including soccer, lacrosse, basketball, baseball, fencing, and attend yoga with her sometimes.

Hewitt's parents are elderly and live in New Jersey, so they are not on her list of helpers. Her ex-husband travels mostly during the week for his work and will have the boys one or two nights on the weekends. 'I live near a few major universities, so I have a network of babysitters for when I have an evening rehearsal or patient. But what happens if the sitter cancels or if I'm sick?' said Hewitt. 'Well, I do have a village of amazing friends. Some are also single mothers; some are married; all work and have children of their own. But they are friends who would loan me 20 dollars if my account were overdrawn, or even more if I needed money to purchase gas or take the boys to the movies. This has unfortunately happened a few times, and is not a great place to be.'

Last year Hewitt had an emergency appendectomy and had to rely on friends for almost a week to help with everything, since she was not able to drive after the surgery. Hewitt arranged friends to take the boys to school and bring them home as well as help her with groceries and around the house. Without her friends, she honestly does not know where she would be. Hewitt said she has in return been there for them: giving financial assistance, helping with their children, helping with work around the house or cooking, and so forth. Hewitt said it does indeed take a village and she is lucky to have the most amazing friends in the world.

Cultivating Friendships in the Community

I believe it's important to cultivate friendships within your neighborhood or community. We have lived in our area for five years, so we have developed friendships with some of the neighbors. One of my neighbors has a young son close in age to Emma; we try to go out once every five weeks or so for a few hours. We check out different restaurants in the city, places we can walk to, and talk about our hectic schedules.

Emma is in daycare only three days a week, so I needed to find additional care for her to prospect for new clients and complete my work assignments. A neighbor has been watching her the other two days in the morning. Relying on a neighbor to babysit has been key. This woman has three kids of her own, two of whom are with Emma when she watches her. She has a son who is Emma's age so they enjoy playing together. She can also watch both girls if I have to attend a late afternoon or evening event.

I am also a member of Philly Social Media Moms, a place for Philadelphia-area mom bloggers to network and socialize. This has been an important vehicle for me to connect with other local mom bloggers, learn more about the blogging world, and the challenges these moms face.

So after five years living here, I have developed friendships with other working moms and stay-at-home moms. Jason and I are happy to be living in Philadelphia, close to all Center City has to offer, but not right in the immediate center. It is a community – and we are here to help each other. I have also connected with parents at the girls' schools on Facebook – this is a good way to stay in contact and updated on activities despite our hectic schedules.

Serena Wadhwa, PsyD, LCPC, CADC, a licensed clinical professional counselor in Chicago, agrees that technology has made it a bit easier to develop a support network. Here are Wadhwa's suggestions:

- Do Internet searches, check out groups on LinkedIn, Twitter, Facebook, or other social media, or even post what you are seeking and see what you get.
- Meetup groups offer supportive networks as well.
- There are groups you can check out at the YMCA, the library, or park districts.
- Check with your local chamber of commerce, hospitals, and social agencies to see what groups they offer.
- Neighbors, friends, and moms with whom you carpool or whose children have play dates with your children – these are all potential network sources.

The point is to figure out what you want support for, and then reach out. 'Most women, in particular, tend to discuss and talk about things on their mind, but do not necessarily seek out solutions or ideas. The opportunity to vent and express themselves is also good. For example, if you are struggling with personal issues, you may want a group where others may be going through something similar, and you feel understood and not alone. You want a network that can offer support,' said Wadhwa. 'Some groups are facilitated by a professional and some are not, so this is something to also consider. Maybe you want a group that offers suggestions and strategies about work or family situations that you're uncertain how to handle. Maybe you're seeking support for your marriage or relationships.'

Another support network to consider is a mentor. 'Mentors

offer specific advice or suggestions on certain things based on their experience or specialization. Maybe you want to find new resources or connections, thus a networking event may be more what you seek,' said Wadhwa. 'So it really depends what you want and what you need. The main point is that you feel you are getting something from it, whether it's connection, an opportunity to vent, a chance to share, get ideas or whatever.'

With the advantage of social media, there are ways to connect with others and receive support in whatever capacity a person seeks, added Wadhwa. 'Most of us can catch a few minutes during the day to connect with others, and that's important. Of course if you are the only person who is initiating this, that may be a different issue.'

Part 4

Work-Life Issues

Chapter 10

Time Management: How Can I Balance It All?

Most career mothers agree that responsibilities overwhelm each day – that there is never enough time to get all tasks accomplished the way they want them. Career moms may strive for perfection in all they do, but soon realize that some things have to give way or they risk their sanity.

I am good at time management, but there are days I over pack my itinerary. For this book, for example, I set a timetable and have met each chapter deadline, much to the joy of my editor. Scheduling has helped me manage my time more efficiently. I allot time for work and home tasks: a half-hour for a conference call, two hours for client updates, two hours at the park with the girls, one hour for lunch, one hour for food shopping, and so forth.

Every day, I evaluate my calendar and the tasks needing to be done. If I have a heavier workweek, I may have to hire a babysitter for late afternoons. If I don't have time to clean the house, then I call our cleaner. We've been using the same house cleaner for over four years who does a wonderful job. It pays to use her service because it would take me more time to do this, and frankly she's much better at it.

Yes, our house is sometimes messy. The girls' toys are not always put away. I turn away from this and cut myself some slack. After all, many evenings I have to return to the computer to catch up on work I could not finish in the afternoon. I love both working and spending time with the girls during the week. Working from home comes with some trade-offs, but I enjoy the daily challenges and adventures with the girls.

Career moms are the ultimate multitaskers, yet they're not too happy about it. Research cited in the December 2011 issue of the *American Sociological Review* reveals that working moms are juggling multiple roles at once – and having a tough time doing so. 'This helps explain why women feel more burdened than men,' says Shira Offer, lead author of the study and an assistant professor of sociology at Bar Ilan University in Israel. 'It's related not only to quantity of time but also to their experience when they multitask.'

Mothers Multitask More than Dads

Both parents reported multitasking at work more than at home, where it was a negative experience. The study's most dramatic finding is that mothers multitask more often than fathers when they do housework – doing dishes while making dinner, for example – and they feel conflicted and stressed about it.

Offer and colleagues looked at data collected from 368 US mothers and 241 fathers in dual-earner, middle- to upper-middle-class families in 1999 and 2000 (when the dot.com bubble burst). The parents held professional jobs and managerial positions, representing a segment that is under time pressures.

The working moms indicated that they multitask 48.3 hours each week, compared with fathers' 38.9 hours. Moms are focusing on more than one thing a head-spinning 43 percent of their waking hours. In terms of housework, moms reported that housework accounts for 53 percent of their multitasking at home, compared with 42 percent for dads; childcare was the focus of at-home multitasking 36 percent of the time for moms and 28 percent for dads.

So on average fathers multitask less often at home, but when they do, they have a completely different experience because they are less likely to engage in housework drudgery. They may do two things at once, but it's less labor-intensive tasks such as talking on the phone while getting dressed.

Offer figures that the findings have everything to do with

social expectations. While today's generation of fathers is expected to be involved in housework and childcare, women often still play a primary role. 'We expect mothers to be good workers who are highly committed to their work, but they are also the ones held accountable for how their children do and how their households are run,' says Offer. 'So they have to multitask. There's no other way to do it.'

In research for this book, I found that women indeed have to take the lead in the household duties. Moms expect their husbands or partners to participate in household duties like diaper changing, cooking, and food shopping. Resentment can build if their partners don't share in these chores.

A June 2011 survey of more than 1,200 mothers by ForbesWoman and the pregnancy website TheBump.com confirmed what moms already suspect: most of these moms resent their partners because they handle far less than their share of the housework and childcare. Most mothers said they feel like single moms, despite being married or living with a partner. I'm sure some moms characterized their husbands as being like teenagers from a prior marriage.

This survey revealed that 92 percent of working moms report feeling overwhelmed by the demands of work, maintaining a household, and parenting; more than 60 percent said they feel like they're managing everything solo. Whether a woman worked professionally or stayed home to take care of the kids made no difference in how the mothers perceived their responsibility for domestic duties.

Both working and stay-at-home mothers said they are mostly in charge when it comes to laundry, shopping, cooking, and cleaning, as well as bathing, feeding, dressing, and entertaining children.

The Weak Economy's Effect

How has the economic downturn affected working mothers' time management? A few work-life experts weighed in:

- Shari McGuire, author of *Take Back Your Time: 101 Simple Tips to Shrink Your Work-Week and Conquer the Chaos in Your Life* (CreateSpace, 2011), thinks the economic downturn doesn't affect their situations – working mothers do it to themselves. 'Working mothers who blame the economic downturn for longer work hours or more pressure are creating the situations for themselves. They tell themselves they need to work longer hours or "I am stressed out,"' she said. 'People are really good at creating worry scenarios in their head and manifesting that story in their life. Then they get to be right – "See, I told you the economy is bad, and I have to work longer hours because of it."'
- The economic downturn has impacted a lot of the women executives known to Karlin Sloan, CEO and author of *Smarter, Faster, Better; Unfear; and Lemonade: The Leader's Guide to Resilience at Work* (Jossey-Bass, 2006), because they are fearful of taking leave or even of sticking up for themselves about issues such as time off, late hours, or working on the weekends. 'I think it's really self-induced pressure in some of them, and it's coming from fear of losing their jobs. More and more women are the main breadwinners in their households, and their salary is critical for getting by,' said Sloan. 'It's hard when we know there are fewer jobs out there and we're not as likely to immediately find new work if we lose our existing job. We can't let the fear get to us!'
- This is a time to pull together as a family. 'You don't need to tell children things that will scare them, but they do have to understand that things may change in what they can do or buy. A family discussion and group effort can be a wonderful boost for family bonding,' said Diana Fletcher, author of *Happy on Purpose: Daily Messages of*

Empowerment and Joy for Women (CreateSpace, 2011). 'Moms need to ask for help and tell everyone why. Children may not like this at first, but when their contribution is recognized and acknowledged they will feel pride in their effort.'

Several mothers shared with me their time management struggles, especially how they solved them or are working on them. Beata Santora, editor of the advice website and podcasting network Quick and Dirty Tips, told me the economic downturn was responsible for her huge life change. She was an editor at a major travel publication in New York. The job allowed her to live a fabulous jet-setting lifestyle. 'My husband and I traveled the world, stayed in fancy hotels, ate at posh restaurants, and generally had fabulous experiences. We talked about having a family someday, but it was hard to walk away from this lifestyle,' said Santora.

Then came 2008 and the crash. Her employer's revenue plummeted, and the magazine had to cut 25 percent of all expenses. Instead of mass layoffs, the magazine management decided to cut back on the hours of many staff, including Santora. She went from full-time to just three days a week, eliminating all travel and associated expenses. It was a huge blow.

Santora talked it over with her husband. They quickly realized that given the circumstances – namely, more free time, no more travel – this was a good time to start a family. It happened almost immediately. Their baby was born in September 2009, just as the economy was recovering somewhat in terms of magazine ad sales. Management brought her back to full-time.

Once she had the baby, Santora realized that working crazy, odd hours, traveling all the time, and making little money were not conducive to this new life. So she found a new, much better paying job with no travel and with a regular 9 a.m. to 5 p.m. schedule.

'The right choice? Yes, of course. But it was a sacrifice. I miss traveling terribly. I miss going out after work with friends; I miss having some disposable income – it all now goes toward our full-time babysitter,' said Santora. 'I miss having independence and freedom. My life is scheduled to odd minutes. I get up at 6 a.m. each day, I go to work at 8:39 a.m., and I come home by 6 p.m. when the nanny goes home. I go to bed at 10 p.m. That's it.'

Jenevieve Fisher, executive director of Educate A Cure, a 501(c)3 that is an international outreach program dedicated to educating children of the world about disease, illness, and disability, said her time management issues include continually checking her email. She has learned to do this after she has checked her number one priority of the day off her list prior to checking her email, or she gets caught up in it for hours.

Another time management issue is homeschooling her four oldest boys. Fisher finds herself putting them off in order to do her work: bills, taxes, phone calls, cooking, cleaning, etc. She has had to make a strict, 15-minute interval schedule for the mornings, in order to accomplish several vital tasks.

Fisher gets sidetracked with phone calls as well. 'If I answer every call I want to answer, I lose the entire day! I have started to use my BlueTooth, decline non-necessity calls, as well as calls from numbers I do not recognize,' said Fisher. 'It's much easier to check the voicemail by BlueTooth, and prioritize, than to answer every call compulsively. My biggest problem with time management is families with a sick child who are calling, emailing, texting, etc. I love to help them, educate them, console them, etc., but I have a very difficult time saying, "No"!'

Fisher now limits phone calls to 20 minutes, and then graciously lets callers know she needs to tend to her own family, and can return the call again or email, within the next two days. 'Emails from families can get out of hand quickly, too. I have Gmail, so no matter how many there are from the same person, they are all streamed together. However, when you have a parent who is at home with a very sick child, they have a lot of time on their hands, and can send countless emails a day. Therefore, I check those emails once a day,' said Fisher. 'Many issues resolve themselves throughout the day, and all I have to do is read them once as they all unfold. It's a nice time-saver!'

The economic downturn has affected Fisher's time. Her husband went from building two homes a year, to now remodeling, doing dirt work, and no new builds, so he is gone a lot. Not having that built-in helper, idea bouncer, and all together supporter to keep her sane has complicated things. His hours are basically 6 a.m. to 8 p.m., which means Fisher gets up at 3 a.m. each day, does her work until 8 a.m., homeschools the boys, etc. until he is home at 8 p.m., and literally goes to bed.

Fisher doesn't work more hours due to the economy, but seems to have to work harder. 'It's more difficult to sell books, because people now want to know exactly what their money is going to get them... there must be a reward for money spent, and the benefit must outweigh the amount. If it isn't presented or represented well, people don't want to take the risk anymore,' she said. 'This is very prevalent in my husband's business, where homeowners are demanding high quality work for a low quality price. They seem to think there are so many people looking for work, that the cost for work done should be much less. It has become increasingly difficult for people to continue to be paid at the level they had been, prior to the economic downturn.'

Fisher is doing things to address the changes, including taking a mini-vacation within driving distance, instead of their typical vacation. Since giving makes everyone feel good, as a family they have decided to spend the time and money they typically would have spent on themselves, to make and deliver sack lunches to homeless people in Seattle. 'It makes us feel better about the situation we are all in. The money is well spent, the time is bonding for our family, and we are truly helping our neighbors,' she said. 'We also spend more time at our home, instead of going out. We have taught our four oldest boys to cook, and be an integral part of preparing meals, so we spend quite a lot of time in the kitchen, and planning meals as well.'

Instead of eating at the local Mexican restaurant on Saturday night, the Fishers take that time and money to make their own Mexican dinner at home as a family. The boys love Chinese night, Italian night, and Sushi night. Fisher loves it because it removes the chef hat a few nights a month, and that makes a difference when she is severely sleep deprived. 'Running my three businesses, my husband's business and a new non-profit, as well as homeschooling, has opened the door of learning for me. I have learned that no matter how little money is coming in, find joy in every day. No matter how much or how little work there is, keep searching for more,' Fisher concluded. 'No matter how little time you think you have to get it done, calmly focus, and the time you get will be enough. Appreciate every moment, because good or bad, we are molded by them, and our children are molded by us.'

Set and Respect Limits

Working mothers need to set limits and respect the limits they set. 'What I mean by that is they need to assess their life and say, "What's important that I must and want to do? And what can I stop doing?" They need to remove the "stop doing" items from their schedule and say no whenever these limit-breakers try to creep back into their schedule,' advised McGuire.

'If they say they will only work 45 hours per week, they need to establish those work hours and walk away when their 45 hours are up – no ifs, ands or buts about it,' said McGuire. 'We teach people how to treat us and when we allow them to schedule a meeting during our non-work hours, we send the message that our schedule isn't so important and we aren't that important.'

Becoming burned out is a choice. McGuire learned the hard

way that our desire to be Superwoman is what can drive us to burn out because that's how she became burned out in 2010. 'We bring that burnout on ourselves by agreeing to do too many projects at the office, leading too many school activities, cleaning the house by ourselves, and so on. Our ego is not our amigo,' she said. 'When I learned this valuable lesson, I found 1,200 hours in my year that I didn't believe existed that allows me to spend more time with my family and enjoying activities that are fun for me.'

Sloan said the first thing moms need to do is to remember that we don't have to be perfect. 'A wonderful colleague of mine who is the mother of three told me this year that she has gone from being a perfectionist to being an "excellentist,"' said Sloan. 'It means she does a "good enough" job in every aspect of her life and doesn't expect that she's going to do everything herself. It really does take a village, and we need help! The more we can build community both at work and at home, the easier our lives can be.'

To prevent burnout, working mothers must be clear on what they want their life to look like and take steps toward achieving that. First, they need to assess what their life currently looks like and what they want it to look like – like a 'before and after' story. 'When they get really excited about the after story, they're ready to take steps toward achieving that after story. Then it's just a process of taking bite-sized steps toward that goal,' said McGuire. For example, if you're on too many committees or boards, determine which one activity brings you the most enjoyment and resign from the rest of the activities.

So McGuire found 1,200 hours in her year and was able to take back her time. Sloan said there are tried and true time-management strategies, such as taking ten minutes every morning to identify the most important things you'll deal with today and this week. Steven Covey's 'first things first' model is a great resource.

Replenish Your Energy

While time management is important, we can also learn to manage our energy, which can be replenished, unlike time. 'Managing our energy means every time we expend our energy, we need to figure out ways to get it back. If you expend all of your energy at work, what do you need to do before going home that will get you your life force back?' asked Sloan. 'Can you call a friend on the way home? When we manage our energy, we end up having more time!'

'Resilience is the most important attribute we can have as working moms – the capacity to bounce back from changes or challenging times,' said Sloan. Research shows that resilience depends on three things: our relationship with ourselves, others, and our external environment. In short, what happens around and to us.

Sloan believes in three things that help her to stay sane as a working mom:

1 Relationship to self: Take time for yourself every single day. Even if it's only five minutes.
2 Relationship to others: Reach out and ask for help, and offer help to other working moms in whatever form you can. We need each other!
3 Relationship to environment: Learn to reframe challenges into opportunities. How can you learn, grow, or develop through experiencing challenges?

Cindy Hamilton, the owner and president of Hamilton Marketing Group in Nashville, Tennessee, spent her time after college building her career in the music industry. She got married in her late twenties and then started a family in her thirties. 'Of course, I bought into the "You can have it all!" mentality that is formed in little girls from the time they have a baby doll and pigtails. Somehow, I just knew I could have a career, a family, and a clean bathroom all at the same time *and* still have time to go to the gym,' said Hamilton.

Then Hamilton's first child was born and everything changed. 'The first few years were like a whirlwind. Drop-off at daycare; meetings, meetings, and more meetings; pick-up from daycare; fix dinner, wash bottles and pack for the next day's drop-off at daycare; and round and round it went,' she said. 'Let alone finding time for laundry, grocery shopping, or scrubbing toilets! That happened on my "days off."'

Around the time her second child was born in 2009, the economy started to take a nose-dive, and the music industry took a major hit. Hamilton was able to move to a part-time position, which helped her and her employer. Over time, she found herself working to pay for childcare. Nearly nothing was left of her part-time paycheck once she paid for daycare.

Starting a Business from Home

In 2010, Hamilton decided to take a leap of faith and quit her corporate job to start a small marketing firm from her home. Over the course of 18 months, it has grown from one client to 12 and continues to grow each month. Hamilton thought this would finally be the solution to having it all.

Not so fast. 'While I love the freedom of being home with my kids, it does come with challenges. Now I have conference calls with clients while locked in my bathroom so they don't hear my 2-year-old melting down in the living room, and I work after my children go to bed or before my family gets up in the mornings so I can still have family time later in the day,' said Hamilton.

'Being a wife, mother, and professional is the biggest challenge in the world no matter your work situation,' she said. However, Hamilton wouldn't have it any other way.

Roz Kirby Walker, a social media marketing strategist, brand consultant, and business development coach based in Nashville, left a high-paying job in corporate America to care for her children, but they still needed her former income amount. Walker started working from home to help supplement her husband's income. It was challenging getting started, so that required her to work long hours building her business.

Walker's kids were 4 years old and 1 year old at the time, and she was homeschooling her oldest. She had to balance her time between being a wife, homeschooling, raising a toddler, doing housework, cooking, and working from home. There never seemed to be enough time and her to-do list was ever growing.

When the economy soured, Walker found it more difficult to find clients because more people were struggling to pay their bills and were cutting back on buying the type of services she offered. She decided to make a change in her business focus and learn a new skill that was more in demand. Walker was then able to create a business that offered marketing services to other businesses and found this to be lucrative even in a down economy.

In addition to learning a new skill and changing her business focus, Walker also had to address her time-management issues. She made a list of all her responsibilities and created a schedule that would allow her focused time on all areas. She also included time in her schedule for interruptions, so that unplanned events would not cause stress. The benefit? She had extra time whenever these anticipated interruptions did not materialize.

Walker enlisted the help of her husband by scheduling two 'work nights' in which he would take the kids out and spend time with them. This gave her four uninterrupted hours to focus on work. She posted her schedule where the family could see it, and she sticks to it as much as possible. By taking these steps, Walker has been better able to manage her time.

I have utilized this technique as well – Jason will take the girls out on the weekend for a few hours so I can catch up on work or write. Being self-employed, I really don't have the option not to work on weekends as I have a flex schedule during the week.

Prioritize Your Life List

Think about overall balance. Is your life balanced in the way you want it to be? 'In order to answer that question, you need to set aside time to prioritize. Not just prioritize your to-do list; you need also to prioritize your life list,' said Fletcher.

What is truly important to you? Family? Career? Relationships? 'This list may change periodically, but a good starting point is to pick the top three for one month. Each day and each week evaluate – are you giving these things the time and attention that they deserve? Are you just saying that these things are important but you are not following up with action?' Fletcher asked. 'Each day may not be balanced with your top three, but over a week's time, there should be balance with your top three. This is just one technique to use.'

Another way to look at this: At the end of your life, what will you look back on and wish you had spent more time on? 'Wouldn't you rather look back and be happy with your choices?' posed Fletcher.

That is a great question to ponder. Later in life, when I look back on all I have done, I envision several books under my name. I procrastinated on writing a book for over ten years. I realized last year that, because I am at the mid-life point, I had better get started. I enlisted the help of a book coach to help me fine-tune the book proposal, table of contents, and sample chapter. Once the publisher's agreement was signed, then I was off and running.

This book is a project I have enjoyed tremendously and a major time commitment. Other authors have used the expression 'it's like giving birth again.'

You would be wise to ask yourself, 'What do I desire to spend my time on and how can I make that happen? What activities can I drop from my current schedule to ensure I meet my new goal?'

Fletcher shared these pointers in closing:

- Moms need to face the reality that they cannot do it all. Instead of trying, again look at what is the most important. That's where you need to spend your time. Not everything is of equal importance.
- One thing that is so important is sleep and down time. Everyone in the family needs this. Cranky children and cranky mommies do not have fun, and it makes it harder on everyone. When everyone has enough sleep, everything will run more smoothly.
- A mom has to learn to say *no*. With practice, it gets easier. Saying *no* to too much is saying *yes* to a happy and efficiently run life. Everyone benefits.
- Moms need to ask for help and hire help.
- Moms need at least 15 minutes of quiet 'alone' time each day to rejuvenate.

Moms have to ask for help and lower their expectations. 'A child will not clean or cook the way you do. That is not what is important. What is important is not wearing yourself out or making the kids anxious and upset. Don't criticize and don't expect family members to read your mind. Be specific in what you need help with,' said Fletcher.

Kids can take turns making dinner when a mom has to work late. 'Peanut butter and jelly sandwiches are a perfectly acceptable dinner,' added Fletcher. 'When you are home, *be* at home with your kids. When you are at work, *be* at work. If you focus on where you are, then your time at home and your time at work will be efficient and well spent.'

Darla DeMorrow, owner of HeartWork Organizing and author of *The Pregnant Entrepreneur* (Blue Tudor Books, 2011), gave up sleep when she became a mom, or at least it feels that way to her. 'Any mom who loves her work is doubly blessed, but we don't get twice the hours in the day. Moms of very young kids (under 6) are in a very hard spot, since little people require constant attention,' she said. 'Keeping a healthy family and a healthy business through that stage is really a huge accomplishment. If you're there, give yourself a pat on the back.'

As a professional organizer, DeMorrow helps herself and others be their best with these time-tamers:

1   Set clear limits on technology. DeMorrow does not take appointments, make calls, or take calls before noon. If she does, the kids are clamoring for her attention or breaking something.

2   Give your kids the gift of sleep. Her kids, now 2 and 4 years old, have extremely regular sleep schedules because she makes sure they do. They go to bed at noon and 7 p.m. every day. DeMorrow never travels during naptime. They are healthier for it, and so is she. Without that, she would not be as consistent or focused in her business.

3   Write it down. Never again ask, 'Now what should I do next?' DeMorrow said she can't rely on her poor memory. A calendar and task list is always with her and captures her every commitment. A family wall calendar simply isn't sufficient for today's entrepreneurial mom.

4   Hire help. This goes beyond hiring a housekeeper or babysitter. DeMorrow hired an assistant. She even hired other professional organizers to help her in her own office from time to time. She has an MBA, and she still hires a CPA. Bring in others so you can focus on what you do best. Even extremely capable and accomplished women can't and shouldn't do it all.

5   Just because you *can* do something doesn't mean you *should*. DeMorrow would love to market more, take more training, network more online and in person, take her kids to the park every day, and volunteer more. Just because she

could do any of these things doesn't mean that she has time or that they fit with her personal or business mission.

6 Stop spinning. Forget what you should be getting done. Do one thing at a time and you can get a lot accomplished. Stop the multitasking madness!

If DeMorrow could change one thing about her day, it would be to get more sleep. Researchers now believe that more and better quality sleep can improve all sorts of things, including promoting weight loss and improving decision-making. DeMorrow is working on it. She's hiring more help, and using Evernote to keep her task list more current and all-encompassing. When she lays her head on her pillow, she rarely thinks, 'Oh, I have to remember to do that tomorrow.'

DeMorrow is still working on creating a strong business that only takes a sustainable amount of energy, and not absolutely all of her energy. She suspects that when her kids are in school full-time, she'll be able to reorganize her business again, and enjoy a more regular work-week without burning the midnight oil.

Chapter 11

Self-Care: How Do I Find 'Alone' Time?

Many working mothers today find it difficult to find enough time for themselves to relax or unwind after a busy workweek meeting deadlines, managing teams, commuting into the office, and so forth. Weekends go by too fast, and most moms can't just take the weekend off away from their kids. The to-do list is endless – grocery shopping, meal preparation, kid birthday parties, and play dates, just to mention a few regular items.

As I write this on a Sunday in February, I have one hour of 'self' time, and this morning I am choosing to spend it at the grocery store. Jason will be gone most of the day on a hike; I lined up a babysitter for an hour and a half so I can also attend a local nutrition seminar. Late this afternoon, I am taking the girls to a Media Moms event or play date at Grow Thru Play, a mix of fun for them (and me, as I look forward to meeting some other local mom bloggers). The girls can run around the play area. If I have enough energy, I will finish writing this chapter tonight. That is my ambitious plan for the day.

Like countless other career moms with young kids, I do not have enough time to myself. I know the situation will change when the girls are older. For now, however, I am putting self-care on the back burner. My first priority is to find some new clients. This takes time and work. Once I win new business, I will breathe a bit easier. Until that happens, I will be in 'full prospecting' mode, emailing past clients and prospects, and searching online ads.

I asked several other working moms how they find rejuvenation time for themselves. Julie McGlynn, an executive at a financial company in Manhattan and mother of 1-year-old twins, Clare and Monica, shared her hectic work schedule. McGlynn moved to the suburbs to have more space for the twins and engage the excellent public school system. They settled on a location because of its proximity to New York. One issue arose afterward: no childcare was available in the area so they settled on putting the twins in daycare in a town about 11 miles north. So a typical day for McGlynn starts at 5 a.m. She gets herself ready for work. Her husband, Damien, is up at 5:30 a.m. At about 5:45 a.m., McGlynn wakes up the twins.

McGlynn gets the girls changed and dressed. They all leave the house at 6:20 a.m. After McGlynn drops Damien off at the train, and after she brings the twins to daycare, she tries to catch the 7:18 a.m. train into Manhattan. She gets to work between 8:30 a.m. and 9 a.m., works a full day, and leaves at 4:55 p.m. to make the 5:17 p.m. train, even though this drives her boss nuts. McGlynn gets back to her community about 6 p.m., collects the twins, meets Damien at the train about 7 p.m., and then shuttles the family home.

Once they are home, they bathe, feed, and dress the girls for bed. 'After that I make their lunch and dinner for the next day, wash their dishes from today, while Damien cooks dinner. We eat and clean up. At about 9 p.m., we sit down,' she said. 'I have about one and a half hours to relax before I go to bed. I like to use the computer, watch television, or read a magazine. I also spend time talking to my husband to ensure that we are on the same schedule and that everything is moving forward on our endless to-do list,' she added.

On the weekends, McGlynn spends most of her time with Clare and Monica. 'I see so little of them Monday to Friday that I love reading them stories, playing with them, and taking long walks with them along the Long Island Sound,' she said. 'I enjoy my Friday and Saturday nights hanging out with my husband. We like to cook and try new wines. It's my favorite part of the week.'

As far as carving out real 'me' time, McGlynn said she hasn't been able to accomplish this. 'I have the train trip in and out of New York to read. I like going to get my hair cut – I find that relaxing. I just wish I had more time to meet with friends, get some exercise, and do a few things for me.'

Because they both have held their jobs, the economic downturn did not have a noticeable impact on their situation. Neither had plans to stay home during this growing-up time; the couple needed to work regardless. McGlynn said the hours away from home and reduced personal-couple time is more a function of living away from her job than the downturn.

'I tend probably like every other working mother to be burned out, tired, and guilty that I don't spend enough time with Clare and Monica. The only thing that helps is the smiles on their faces every day when I pick them up,' she said. 'I also have learned to slow down – you can't do everything. One thing at a time and be super-organized.'

Shanetris Campbell, author of *I Am Not My Father's Daughter* (Publicly Owned Publishing Company, 2011), said that when she takes a good look at her life – mother of a 9-year-old, owner of three businesses, full-time caregiver, full-time chef, full-time taxi, tutor, mommy, project manager, writer, author, promoter, entre-preneur – it's no wonder her mornings greet her with a panic attack. She has so many things to manage and set straight on a daily basis it gets overwhelming, fast.

Campbell said she is in the most delicate part of her life – shaping her career and business. 'Life to me, in this moment, is a great, wide-open, blank canvas and guess who gets to play? Me. It's great and full of potential, but that canvas at times can look splattered with dark hues at the edges,' she said. 'This is why balance and a positive mindset are necessary. I've realized that it's all in the way I look at it.'

Stealing 'Me' Time

As it relates to 'me' time, Campbell has adopted the purloin method for herself. 'The beauty of me stealing my time is that it gives me the opportunity to work for my chosen escapades. Yes, I am guilty of making them fun and naughty in the cash arena,' she said. 'I complete a deadline and for celebration I'll treat myself to a spa day or splurge meal at a place I've been craving to go to. It seems planned, but it can create a future struggle for my single-mom bank account.'

In regards to the perilous economy, Campbell said it's been the scariest rollercoaster ride she's ever been on. 'In the beginning, I held strong to the belief that the media was making these dramatic stories to scare the "be-jesus" out of people and force us into a political position. They knew we'd be there in front of the television by 7 p.m. waiting for them to give us a gleam of hope. We got the brutal facts. But they didn't often dispense the hope. I thought it was worse than a fierce domestic relationship – they knew we'd be back for more. And we were.'

The truth really hit home when she took her travels out of the country a little more seriously. In most countries Campbell visited, she had enough knowledge of the local language to get around, engage, learn, and discover. She met with others and found out what they were experiencing in their local context. She realized that it was a lot worse than she had expected. Although it seemed that the other countries had more than we did, the struggle and hardships were much the same.

The recession scared Campbell into doing things that she'd not previously done, such as writing a book about her life and producing it with a team she handpicked. 'I would've never imagined that I could do it, alone. It took a change in my way of thinking about myself, a change in the woman I was, before I could aspire to be the different woman I had envisioned,' said Campbell. 'And with the economic downfall, it's what has challenged me to move beyond what I thought I knew and redis-cover who I am today. I now have the opportunity to create a legacy for my son and me.'

Campbell believes there are several degrees of burnout – mild burnout to medium burnout to Code Red Burnout. 'There is quite a difference between multitasking and attempting to be Superwoman. A mother still has to have her hands in her daily mommy duties; being an entrepreneur calls for another set of skills and a big chunk of time for developing or even maintaining a company,' she said. 'How a mother can accomplish both things is magical, if you ask me. Burnout for a working mother is a predictable outcome, not a bittersweet luxury.'

In all, Campbell loves her life and has learned how to work within her own limits, love the successes both as a mom and a new business owner, and create more from them. She knows that stealing her 'me' time is necessary or else she'd lose her mind. She's learned to work with what she has until she can make more or better. The best lesson she has ever learned is to be present – in the moment. And when she does this, she realizes that right now is always perfect.

The weakened economy has left me feeling less secure financially. I seem to have to work harder to find – and keep – clients. It has made me a bit apprehensive at times. As I've mentioned before, I love self-employment and running my own business. When a business or author signs a long-term contract with me, I get such a rewarding feeling. It puts my mind at ease and allows me a break from marketing my services.

I would love to spend money on bigger, more exotic family vacations, but that is not in the cards. I have grown to love trips to my parents' beach house when the weather is warm – that is always a treat for the girls. Twice a year I visit a girlfriend in Manhattan for the weekend – that is always exciting. I know the situation will change, but for now I just need to appreciate the moments I can get away.

The economic downturn affects working moms' situations by making families feel particularly vulnerable, 'feeling like they can't take time out for themselves because they should be spending more time looking for work, keeping the job they have, or spending more time with their children,' said Lisa Haisha, Hollywood counselor and humanitarian. 'This economic downturn is actually the time when they need more time by themselves, because alone time helps you find the answers that can help get you out of the situation.'

'It causes people's Impostors – their dark side – to come out; they get short-tempered, wake up stressed or angry, and take it out on family members or friends,' Haisha said. 'Take a deep breath and keep your Impostors in check by responding to them, but without reacting. The more you can get a grasp on not reacting, the more empowered you will be and the better your day will go.'

'The downturn has had a massive effect on people's lives,' agreed UK-based Lianne-Carla Savage, a work-at-home mom of two under 3 years of age. Savage incorporated her first company when her eldest turned 2 and the youngest was three months old. Now she advises other mompreneurs. 'Jobs are in short supply and increasingly more is asked of employees in order to fulfill their roles. The stress is affecting everyone, and more people are being diagnosed with depression. Now more than ever is the time to invest in the little things that boost emotional well-being,' she said. 'Sometimes there is no option but to work overtime; some people find they are working second jobs or taking the leap by starting a business alongside their day job. It can be tiring and overwhelming at times.'

Interestingly, it appears to have caused couples to divide more equally the household chores and parenting activities – a small silver lining, perhaps, said Cynthia Calvert, founder and principal of Workforce 21C. 'More women stayed in the paid workforce and more went back into the paid workforce as a result of a disproportionate percentage of men who were laid off. I don't have hard data on this, just anecdotes and media stories. What I've been hearing about is that men who were laid off are assuming more of the family work,' she said.

Another anecdotal, media-reported phenomenon leads Calvert to believe, however, that the downturn – and men doing more family work – hasn't necessarily translated to more self-care or free time for women. 'People who retained their jobs often had to work (and continue to have to work) very hard to do the work of the people who were laid off. Longer hours and being on call when at home has made leisure time more scarce,' she added. 'This scarcity makes it all the more important for women to deliberately plan and negotiate time for themselves to prevent burnout.'

Physical and Mental Health Is Vital

Mothers can carve out time for themselves – which they must do for physical and mental health reasons, and to be a better parent. Calvert said this requires four things:

1   Women need to share family and home obligations with a partner or spouse. Women have made great strides toward equality in the workplace, but not at home. 'Household chores and parenting responsibilities need to be divided equally,' Calvert said. 'If some chores can be outsourced, all the better – but both partners need to have responsibility for setting up and monitoring the outsourced work. Women will never be equal at work or have time for themselves until they can achieve equality at home.'

2   Sharing chores and parenting at home requires not only men (or partners) to shift their mindsets but also women to shift their mindsets as well. Calvert said women need to give over the duties completely – no monitoring, no nagging, no correcting, no guilt, and no profuse thanks. Men (or partners) are not 'helping' – they are equally responsible.

3   Shift one's mindset away from guilt for time away. Mothers

need to realize that they are better mothers who can be more present and emotionally available to their children if they have some down time. They also make better role models for their children when moms model relaxation and self-care.

4 Finally, carving out time requires planning and cooperation. The spouses or partners need to share calendars so that each person's free time can be scheduled – and both can commit to making it happen for each. Planning for the free time makes such time more likely to happen.

As footnotes to these four elements, Calvert recommends working moms get more sleep – you'll be more efficient and accomplish tasks in less time. Also, trade play dates with a friend – she will watch your children, then you watch hers at another time. This is a good solution for single parents.

Calvert's suggestions for reclaiming your time:

- *Give up perfection.* Families can thrive on simple meals, toys can lie around the house until the weekend, and dust bunnies never killed anyone.
- *Train your children to be helpful* from a young age: pick up toys, set and clear the table, help load the dishwasher, etc.
- *Do your shopping online,* but in a focused way that doesn't eat up the time you're saving. Clothes, birthday presents, school books, food, beauty items, cleaning supplies and more are all available on the web.
- *Pay your bills online* and automate as many payments as possible.
- *Say no to requests to volunteer.* This can be a tough recommendation for many women, so a budget approach works best. Think in advance how much time you are willing to give to volunteer activities, and limit your participation to activities that are not too draining on your time or energy.

- *Set up systems to organize everything.* Investing some time and energy into this now can save many hours and relieve many pains each week.
- *Everything should have a place* – outerwear, sports equipment, toys, craft supplies, books, bills, mail, school work, school forms – to make cleaning a snap and to eliminate time spent searching for things.
- *Encourage your children to eat school lunches.*
- *Limit your children to two extra-curricular activities each,* and get them interested in doing the same activities (or practice arenas) at the same time as their sibling(s), whenever the activities involve transportation.

Business-Home Boundaries

Natalie Bradley, owner of www.BrideAttraction.com, has a 4-year-old girl (who's still at home for now), and she also runs a business working with over 20,000 wedding professionals around the world on how to market and sell to brides. She has had to create strong boundaries between business and home life, especially because she owns a home-based business. 'It can be tricky at times, but I refuse to check email over the weekends. I also do not work on (most) Mondays or Fridays, and I take at least one week off per month to run errands, catch up, and do crafts and art,' said Bradley. 'This is family and personal time to get things done, have extra fun, and do things I want to do, too. The biggest issue I've found when I did not carve out time for myself or my family was that I put everyone else as a priority in front of myself. I have to honor these boundaries, or I burn out and become very unpleasant to be around!'

Bradley told me her business is making a lot more money during this economic shift and so are her clients. Bradley teaches marketing and sales based on her values of creating a life of freedom, not slavery to work. Bradley has actually gone from working five days a week to three within the past year, and taking more time off in general. Admittedly, this makes their lives different than most other families.

'We are very careful of what we watch or read so that we don't get consumed with all the negativity around the economy. It helps me stay focused on knowing that this is my reality and even though the world is going through a major shift, I have options in how I want to live and work,' she said. 'My clients who are successful are the same way. It sounds very Pollyanna, and it is. That's what works for me!'

Of course, there are times when Bradley pushes on a huge launch or has busier weeks, but she listens to her gut and intuition. If she needs a break and feels burnout coming, then she takes time off. No exceptions. 'I've hated my business in the past and didn't listen to my body telling me to slow down. And not listening took its toll. A lesson learned from the past is always to listen to your body and your gut, even if it doesn't feel like the "responsible" action to take,' she added. 'Make sure your business or your work environment is set up to support this, and have a business model that continues to make you money while you rest. It makes life a lot easier and a lot more fun!'

'As mothers, we often find ourselves placing the needs of others before our own needs. Yet we all need to learn to recognize the importance of personal fulfillment,' said Savage. 'Being a working mother delivers the opportunity to rediscover our identities. In the whirlwind of work, however – you know: childcare, deadlines, school pick-ups, parents' evenings, overtime and more – it's no wonder many working mothers find themselves overwhelmed and unfulfilled. Where is the time for you?'

Savage's answer is to prioritize your own needs. This is something she personally does as soon as her two have gone to bed. She found herself in a cycle of hitting 7 p.m. and having a huge list of things she must still do on that evening. That was a cycle she needed to break. Whatever housework she needs to do comes just before bedtime or after she's invested time in herself.

'For one, it re-energizes me so I can hit the ground running on my evening's to-do list. Secondly, it's easy to get distracted when you are pottering away at things, and "getting round" to spending time on yourself just doesn't happen,' said Savage. 'Time for you doesn't have to be a huge event. Something as simple as spending a few minutes polishing your nails, half an hour of yoga, or cracking open that book you've not got around to finishing can be a massive boost.'

Take a lunch break. 'If you don't step back from what you're doing and make sure that your body is getting everything it needs, you will burn yourself out, and you will be less productive for the afternoon. You may have gained a work activity and used it well, but if you are under par for the next four to five hours it will have cost you time in the long run,' said Savage. 'You know what that leads to – missed deadlines and always working overtime to catch up. It's a vicious circle that you have to take yourself off right away.'

'Self' time doesn't just happen – it takes work. Yet the rewards are immense. The time Savage has for herself fluctuates a lot. 'Despite the cool calm and collected surface, I am human after all and occasionally I do get burned out. As a mother, business-woman, and student, my day-to-day activities really do vary. There are times that I don't spend enough time on myself – maybe I have an exam coming up, a sick child, or a marketing piece I need to get finalized to a deadline,' she said. 'The trick comes when you begin to recognize that burnout is happening and you do something about it, even if that means doing nothing at all. Whip off the halo, hop off the pedestal, stop doing every-thing – and take care of what needs to be done. After all, every-thing else is optional.'

Spend 15 Minutes Outside

Rebecca P. Cohen, author of *15 Minutes Outside: 365 Ways to Get*

Out of the House and Connect with Your Kids (Sourcebooks, 2011), offered several ways a working mom can carve out time for herself. She recommends taking time for yourself each day in these 15-minute increments:

- *Step outside at work.* 'Take a brisk walk, sit on a bench and look at the clouds, or close your eyes and feel the warmth of the sunshine and take a few breaths. You'll be amazed how giving yourself space during 15 minutes can feel like a mini-vacation,' Cohen said.
- *Take turns with your spouse.* 'Each day at home, give each other 15 minutes to decompress. He can take the kids, and you can clear your mind. Take a stroll around the block and count your blessings, sit and journal to let go of the challenges of the day, or do a small chore like sweeping the stoop, which can be therapeutic,' Cohen said. 'If you're a single mom, find a neighbor who can be a mother's helper each day to give you a break.'
- *Stroll with your child.* 'If your child is young enough, they can ride in a stroller and you can get some exercise. Even if your kids are older,' Cohen said, 'you can walk or ride bikes together. Fifteen minutes outside will be a stress release valve for everyone in the family.'
- *Use nap time.* While her kids napped in their strollers, Cohen tinkered in the garden, snoozed on a deck chair beside them, or had a cup of tea and read the paper. Use nap time to nourish yourself.

To claim alone time and avoid burnout, Cohen said, ask for help and have compassion for yourself. You don't need to be perfect. You need to take care of yourself so you can take care of your kids. After Cohen tried to do too much on too little sleep with her first son, she made sure to ask for lots of help from family and friends with her second. She was much better rested, and her second baby was much more calm because she made self-care a priority.

Cohen's boys are now 7 and 9 years old, and she still makes trade-offs between doing everything and just enough so that her family and she are healthy and happy. Maybe the house doesn't have to be tidy all the time – she'd choose her 15 minutes outside for her and her family over a picture-perfect house any day.

'The stress of everyday life can take its toll on anyone unless we make self-care a priority,' said Cohen. 'Time outside for you and your family is a great way to make time stand still and appreciate the beauty, no matter how small, that is right in front of us.'

Set a Schedule for Sunday Night

Haisha recommended working moms carve out a Sunday night schedule ahead of time, and then stick to it. 'Make meals Sunday night for the kids, like having hamburgers, soup, something that will last for a few days in the fridge,' she said. 'If an emergency comes up, that's fine, go ahead and take care of it, but make sure you get that "alone" time later.'

'Parcel out your days in blocks,' Haisha said, 'and then arrange your day by moving those blocks around. Whatever time your child has to be up, get up a half-hour earlier and have a ten-minute meditation on what you'd like your day to be like.'

To ensure alone time and avoid burnout, Haisha shared three tips:

- *Delegate, delegate, delegate.* Get off the idea that you have to be a Martyr-Mom, and ask for help. Have someone come in and babysit for you even if it's for three hours a week and do a trade if you can't afford it. You could swap babysitting with another parent so that each of you have a night off.
- *Get out once a week* with your friends or by yourself or with your spouse. One night a week is adult-night only – your kids will survive.

- *Do something positive for yourself every day* – it can be meditation, a walk, a bath. 'Create your day by waking up a little before everyone else so that you can take control of your day rather than helplessly watching it unfold. When you're empowered with your Authentic Soul, your day naturally goes well,' she said. 'If you are letting your Impostors run you, and play the victim, then things will spiral out of control and you'll lose where the hours in your day go.'

Chapter 12

Work: Where Do I Take My Career?

Working mothers need periodically to evaluate their careers and determine their best growth opportunities. This decade, more women will be seen altering their jobs to allow more time for their families. How can the two trends happen? With superb technology available, women can complete training on their own time, work from their homes, and spend less time commuting or office dwelling.

Do you know where your career is headed? Are you going through the motions on the job? Or do you have a set career plan? Is a corporate role or entrepreneurship right for you?

Times have changed and will continue to do so. In the Great Recession, three-quarters of the eight million jobs lost had been held by men. The worst-hit industries were predominantly male: construction, manufacturing, and finance. In 2010, for the first time in US history, the workforce tipped toward women, who hold a majority of the nation's jobs.

In the aftermath of the Great Recession, men's and women's roles have become less defined; so-called traditional male and female roles in the family have become, well, less traditional and more equal when it comes to jobs, household duties, and childcare. With many husbands unemployed, more women have assumed the role of breadwinner, while the number of men tending the home has increased. Stay-at-home men have struggled with this new role and with not being the main source of income. Meanwhile, many women still have to adjust to earning lower wages than men and face a tougher time advancing to the highest positions within a company.

Yet women can work around these obstacles in creative ways. This past year, for example, I evaluated my business services and concluded I would like to expand into ghostwriting books and managing social media for other businesses. Writing this book has certainly opened my eyes to new opportunities and ways to generate additional income. I have enjoyed blogging on working-mother topics and will continue to do so. I plan to attend blogging seminars and workshops to learn more about the trade. I see several more books in my future as well. That is where I predict my career going.

Several mothers spoke to me about how they created careers to make more room for their families. Nicole Feliciano, editor and founder of Momtrends.com, left the traditional office environment to create a work experience that was customized for the needs of her family. At first, she started freelancing and was working about 15 hours a week. She added more clients as her first daughter got older and as she became more confident in her parenting skills.

Soon, she had ramped up to 20 or more hours a week with deadlines set by her editors. All those deadlines were a big part of the reason she launched her own site. Feliciano wanted to work when and where she wanted. Now as her own boss, she sets her own erratic, crazy schedule. But it works for her.

Follow Your True Calling

Feliciano's advice? Follow your passions. 'If work feels like play, and if you have a great team surrounding you, then it's a lot easier to live without huge paychecks. When you do encounter success, don't see it as a fluke – study the cause of the success to see whether you can replicate it,' said Feliciano. 'Our event business surprised me with its earning power. If I didn't take a moment to analyze it, then I might have missed out on a great opportunity.'

Give yourself permission to fail. 'Balance, perfection... they don't exist. Master letting go of your preconceived notions of success. Success for me is about creating a brand that has value.

Success means I saw when and where I work, and how I can put my family first,' added Feliciano. 'There are so many things I have failed at; I just pick myself up and keep on trucking. Be confident that your work is important and that it is important for your family to see you as more than a mom.'

Louisa Leontiades, CEO of Investment Impact, an online consultancy in the UK, noted the saying that 'necessity is the mother of invention.' This is certainly true in her case. Through prejudice and an outdated corporate system, she was neither able to get time off with her newborn daughter nor get any maternity benefit. So she had to find a way to work and take care of her infant at the same time.

'By transforming my expertise into an online consultancy that is delivered in work packages as opposed to working defined hours, I was able to work around breastfeeding and chaotic sleep patterns, thereby earning enough for me to continue to be by her side,' said Leontiades. 'It wasn't easy, and my mission became to build a web platform to give this power to others who needed the same flexibility – both men and women.'

Leontiades offered suggestions for other women to reshape their careers in these tough economic times:

- Transforming technology now touches our lives on a daily basis. Shared knowledge and the power of communication are available to us like never before. Take advantage of this to reach out and connect. Women are phenomenal at doing this. They build relationships, which are much more powerful than simple networks.
- Don't be a sacrifice (or burnt-out offering) for your family. They are precious and amazing, but not more so than you.
- Social media is important for your business, but monitor your time usage. For example, Facebook is great but don't let it consume all of your online time, which could be used for other purposes, such as reshaping your career. So many

services allow you to work flexibly and externalize all the expertise you have, but never display in your day-to-day job.

How can mothers take their careers to the next level – even with active home lives? 'Therein lies the rub. It takes sacrifice,' said Leontiades. 'And that's why taking your career to the next level has to involve your passion – because you have to enjoy reshaping your career despite the sacrifice of your free time that you're making. Dream your ideal life, and then work toward it.'

Flex Jobs Increase

How has the economic downturn affected working mothers' situations? Several experts shared with me what they have seen. Sara Sutton Fell, a mother of two young boys and the CEO and founder of FlexJobs.com who has spent 15 years in the employment industry, said from what they've seen, more women are opting out of the traditional employment structure in favor of flexible work opportunities, either with a company or as a self-employed professional.

According to the *American Sociological Review*, only about 8 percent of women leave the workforce entirely while they're raising children. The vast majority go back to work within a year. 'But with the huge growth in the availability of flexible jobs over the last several years – and the increased awareness of them through media outlets like Working Mother and websites like FlexJobs.com – working mothers seem to be trading in traditional 9 a.m. to 5 p.m. (or 6 p.m. or 7 p.m.) workdays in favor of flexible schedules, and we know for sure that more employers are offering more flexible options in order to retain this large segment of the workforce,' said Fell.

Jill Salzman, the founding mom of The Founding Moms and author of *Found It: A Field Guide for Mom Entrepreneurs* (Piggott Press, 2012), runs an organization that helps moms get down to business in the world of entrepreneurship. She's seen a lot more women move toward self-employment. 'It's an incredible time to start a business, and those moms who have capitalized on it are seeing great results. And they're joining The Founding Moms to better themselves and trade advice, info, and tips to better their companies, too. In the last two years, we've had over 2,000 women join us!' Salzman said.

The tough economy has been really good for mompreneurs, such as Noelle Abarelli, author and founder of *The Smart Mompreneur* (Gandia Communications, 2009). Why? 'Because employers have increasingly been turning to freelancers and contract workers like me as a way to support business initiatives while cutting costs. My clients have not had budgets to hire full-time employees during this downturn, but they have often been able to find funds to hire freelancers for short- and mid-term projects,' said Abarelli. 'I truly don't believe there has ever been more opportunity for self-employed individuals who can fill gaps existing in the corporate arena.'

The US unemployment rate is still high (8.3 percent as I write this chapter, with over 14 million former workers still un- or under-employed). Jason and I don't see an overwhelming number of work opportunities in our respective fields. As I mentioned earlier, he's in finance, one of the toughest-hit industries. I am competing for new contract work and hope to land additional clients soon. I remain committed to self-employment, with no plans to return to a full-time job. With over ten years of communications experience, I am confident in my abilities to deliver results for clients.

When it gets tight financially for us, we buckle down and cut expenses where we can. A vacation is on hold for us at the moment. Since Jason loves to cook, we can save money not dining in restaurants. We can also have an out-of-town relative babysit while they are visiting.

For me, flexible work is paramount. I have molded my career

around the girls' schedules. I enjoy picking them up from school and spending some time with them at the park or library before dinner. That means I have to catch up on computer work at night, but I don't mind – that is what I've carved out for myself. I enjoy having a mix of clients.

If you are a business owner, who is your clientele? You need to have a diverse base of clients in order to remain in business. I've been in situations where I've relied on one or two clients as the sole source of income. When that work was completed, I was left scrambling to find replacement work. It was stressful and not fun.

If I can predict my future income for the next five or six months, then that puts my mind at ease somewhat. As mentioned earlier, I get a great sense of satisfaction when I sign a new client for six months. My most rewarding career experiences have been with long-term clients rather than businesses that have hired me for just one short-term project.

In 2003, Abarelli walked away from an exciting career in international marketing to achieve more balance in her life. She founded a marketing consultancy, and after five years of running her own business, she realized she was spending much of her time informally coaching young women and new moms who were looking to pursue their own entrepreneurial dreams.

Abarelli took time out to research and write an e-book for mompreneurs, and shortly after, she launched a series of coaching programs aimed at helping other women pursue freelance success.

Work-Life Decisions

Today, Abarelli continues to work within her marketing consultancy while also writing, speaking and coaching. She innately understands a mom's need for an intellectual outlet that complements the sometimes tedious task of child-rearing. The goal of her work is to make balancing motherhood and a fulfilling career a little easier and a lot more enjoyable through creativity and practical strategy.

After having a baby, Deborah Sweeney realized she needed to improve her work-life balance and go back to work. She went in-house with one of her clients, MyCorporation. Shortly thereafter, MyCorporation was acquired by Intuit. She was tagged to run the company under Intuit's name, a great opportunity, but nonetheless a loss of that work-life balance she was looking for (also known as control and end-result decision-making).

This all came in tandem with the economy beginning to head into decline. Instead of sticking with life as-is, Deborah decided to take on more responsibility. She wanted to grow the business in a way that industry giant Intuit wasn't able to do. So, as of October 2009, Deborah became 100 percent owner and CEO of MyCorporation and remains great partners with Intuit to this day.

When Sweeney had her first son, she was a partner in a law firm. After about four months, she realized that it would be very difficult to maintain full-time partnership at a firm while having sufficient time to spend with her son. Fortunately, her husband and her mom had flexible careers, so between the three of them, they were making it happen.

It was stressful, though. Sweeney was presented with an opportunity to go in-house and work a more flexible schedule – Mondays and Fridays from home and shorter days on Tuesday through Thursday. This was the perfect opportunity for her. 'When the business I was working for was acquired by Intuit, the flexible schedule became a bit less flexible, but I was still able to maintain a semblance of work-life balance. Ultimately, when given the opportunity, I bought the business out from Intuit,' said Sweeney. 'This was the biggest blessing of my life. While I work a lot, the business has been growing and I have a team of over 40 employees. I have worked hard at enabling others to succeed and to take more responsibility in the business. This has given me the freedom to be very involved in my sons' lives!'

Fortunately, Sweeney said the times seem to be improving. 'With that said, negotiating flex schedules at the outset of a career or job change is very important. Communication is critically important,' she said. 'Also, if you are good at something in particular, it has become more commonplace for women to start their own businesses – whether it's consulting in your area of expertise or working with partners who can share the work load.'

Prove Your Contributions

Hard work does not go unnoticed. If you are in a corporate position, Sweeney said, then it's often about proving yourself. 'If you're a great contributor while you're at work and you make yourself "available" when you're home (even if you're with your kids), most companies will be amenable to a more flexible schedule. Companies love productive people with a great outlook,' she noted. 'Keep a positive approach to your work – don't get so harried that you become the woman who's too distracted to work.'

If you own your own business, then make sure you have the right team. Have people on your team whom you can trust in your absence. 'Don't try to do it all yourself. Having support is one of the most important facets in the success of a woman in business,' said Sweeney.

Sweeney has been fortunate to have her husband and mom, who support her. Because her husband owns his own business, he shares the load. It is a great opportunity for her husband to be involved in their children's lives, and also to share with their boys the importance of both parents working and still being involved in the day-to-day adventures. She likes the fact that her boys are proud of their mom and her career.

Marla Barch, a senior loan officer in the Chicago area and single mother of two young children, worked as a paramedic where neither the hours nor the pay were conducive to raising a child on her own. Initially, she had family step in about half-time to help raise her first child, while she continued to work for modest wages that still did not provide the life she wanted for her child. When her second child was born, she stopped working for a year and spent that year researching careers, seeking flexibility and a higher income.

Barch quickly discovered that most women working from home fell into one of two categories. Either they had built up seniority in their company and therefore were able to take their work home or they were a second income in the house and were participating in direct sale companies (Mary Kay, etc.) for a little extra money. Neither of these situations worked for her.

Barch decided becoming an entrepreneur was her only option. She began researching business ideas and writing business plans. Then, through continued networking, she met her new job: a mortgage loan officer. This job had 100 percent flexibility regarding her time and location and high income potential because this job was 100 percent commission based.

While the commission has been a challenge, especially with some of the trying years in the market, Barch would never exchange the career choice. The flexibility has allowed her to parent how she'd like and be available to her children. She never has to worry about taking a sick day from work when her kid has a fever. 'I'm glad to volunteer to chaperone field trips. My children have never had to attend before or after school programs. I've never missed any of my son's after school basketball games,' Barch said. 'As a result of my career choice, I've also learned about real estate investing and now earn extra income from flipping and renting foreclosures after buying and fixing them up.'

Barch said young women should be counseled on career choices that have flexibility for parenting before they get into the career world and have spent years and possibly decades building a career that is inflexible when they decide to start a family.

Few careers offer the kind of flexibility and income potential that parents need to have the balance they would like, she added. The careers that she has found that meet both criteria of flexibility and income potential include sales, entrepreneurial ventures, and investing. 'The trade-off of having the flexibility is giving up the stable income. Most careers that allow you flexibility are paid as commission or business profit,' said Barch. 'While both of these are wildly unpredictable, they also offer the greatest possible returns if you are successful in your line of work.'

Advance Your Career

So how can mothers take their careers to the next level – even with active home lives? Fell said if you're working, consider asking your current employer for a change to your schedule – whether that be the option to telecommute, work flexible hours, a compressed workweek, or go part-time. 'Make a solid case for changing your schedule and see if they'd allow some flexibility. If not, it's time to find a job that does allow flexible work options,' she said.

Legitimate jobs exist in all types of professions. 'The most important thing is to evaluate your wants and needs – what do you want out of your career and family? What are your absolutely must-not-miss activities at home (dropping your kids at school, attending their plays, being home with them when they're sick, and so forth)?,' said Fell. 'How can you make time for these activities and still have a meaningful career? Most of the time, having a flexible schedule will allow working mothers to balance work and home life.'

Fell said the next step is to find a professional-level job that is in line with your career ambitions but that also allows for a flexible schedule. At FlexJobs, which specializes in flexible job listings, they've seen a 400 percent increase in job openings which offer flexibility since 2007. Now is a fantastic time for working mothers to find a flexible job.

In short – just do it. 'We spend a lot of time worrying about the what-ifs of the situation, but if you are committed to making more time for your family, then it's time to approach your boss about a flexible schedule or telecommuting or working part-time or whatever would make this goal happen for you,' said Fell. 'When we speak to people after they've made the move to a flexible work arrangement, or changed jobs entirely to one that supports their work-life balance through flexibility, they never regret the move. In fact, it seems their only regrets are that it took them so long to make the change.'

Salzman's advice for career moms is to make lists. 'It's the best way to stay organized and on top of everything – kids and careers included. There are myriad ways to do it now, from plain old sticky notes to computer programs like Tadalist.com or the Evernote app,' she said. 'And since we're so mobile these days, staying on top of everything can present even more of a challenge – so pick your go-to list style and keep it up.' Sound too simple? It's helped Salzman build three separate business, one of which she sold last year. She could credit her strong work ethic, sales, or luck, but really – it's in the lists.

There are two things any woman must do in order to make the move from full-time careers to career with family time, said Salzman. First, figure out your creative outlet, that idea that inspires you and may even prevent you from sleeping at night. Something that really excites you and will get you out of bed every morning. Whatever that something is, build a company around it and make sure you can do it full-time and still love it.

Second, find out if there's a market for it before you fully dive in. Go to meetups and coffees and parks and talk to other people. Find out if they'd buy what you want to sell, whether it's a service or a product. If you have that 'something,' and if there's a market for it, then you're in business. You get to be your own boss, create your own schedule, and make as much time for your family as you want.

Abarelli told me the key is making your career a top priority and scheduling time to focus on it. 'Whether you own your personal business or work for a corporate giant, you need to schedule time for work and time for being a mom. Women are really good at multitasking, so we're often tempted to try to juggle too many tasks at once,' she said.

Abarelli finds that she produces her best work when she is fully focused on the task at hand. She works from home, so as a rule, she tries not to work when her kids are up and about. She has set her office hours according to the kids' school schedules and occasionally schedules additional work tasks during hours that they are asleep. These boundaries have helped her be successful at work and at home.

For most moms Abarelli knows, a 9-to-5 career doesn't really suit a lifestyle filled with carpools, colds, and summers off. In fact, a recent survey of almost 2,500 high-achieving women conducted by Sylvia Ann Hewlett found that 37 percent of women stop working for a period, or temporarily 'opt out' of the workforce after having children.

For many of us, however, quitting a job and staying home with no income potential isn't an option, and for that reason, Abarelli said many women are starting their own businesses. While entrepreneurship in general is a common option, in Abarelli's opinion the type of business offering the best combination of flexibility, ease of entry, low risk, minimal start-up capital and high income potential is a freelance business.

'A freelancer is any person who independently performs services or completes work assignments for one or more clients. These clients have the right to control only the final result of the freelancer's work, rather than the specific means used to get the work done,' said Abarelli. 'In essence, a freelancer is the proprietor of his or her own service-based business.'

Abarelli thinks a freelance business is one of the fastest and smartest ways women today can mix their desire to have kids and a career. Why?

1 Virtually everyone has a service to offer. Whether it be designing websites, writing press releases, training users on a new software system, planning events, advising start-up firms on how to raise venture capital, illustrating books, ghostwriting, filling out tax returns, providing legal advice or helping entrepreneurs design and engineer new products, each one of us has a marketable skill that can serve as the foundation for a service-based business.

2 Freelance businesses generally require minimal capital to start. There is no inventory required and no need to hire employees. In many cases, a freelance business can be started for less than $1,000 – the cost of a computer and a set of business cards.

3 Once launched, most freelance businesses can be run from home, which offers numerous advantages for today's women – including low overhead, tax deductions, savings on clothes and commutes, and most importantly, the flexibility to be home when our children are sick, heartbroken or just need a hug.

Conclusion

I learned a lot of valuable lessons by writing this book. Here are some key pointers you can take away to best care for yourself, spouse, and your babies or toddlers.

It's vital for you as a mom not to be a martyr. Take time to care for yourself and find healthy ways of coping with your stress. Build in some space between work and home. These could be small steps like taking a walk or exercising before you walk in the door, or finding a quiet place to sit still for just 15 minutes such as a coffee shop or park.

When speaking with working women, I heard several themes mentioned: money burdens or concerns, work pressures, infrequent companionship, and apportionment of household duties. New mothers struggle with the transition to parenthood – lack of sleep, new responsibilities, less 'self' time, hormones out of sync, and so on. This can easily result in disagreements with your spouse or partner, and unaddressed issues can simmer and get heated.

Unfortunately, many couples with babies fall into the pattern of attacking each other as they don't know effective coping methods for dealing with the stress. If you find your relationship is getting volatile, then it's time to follow the advice in Chapter 2 or, better yet, talk to an outside counselor or therapist.

These challenging economic times have changed the advice some finance experts offer. One expert advocated that you cut your spending down to 65 percent 'needs,' 20 percent 'wants,' and 15 percent 'savings,' for example. Many advisers are against accumulating debt more now than ever.

Couples should create a budget. Sit down with your spouse or partner, and put your expenses and financial goals on paper. Be realistic, and make sure that following the budget won't require too much effort. Find a certified financial planner in your area who will prioritize your goals, put money figures next to them, and show you how to attain them.

For many working moms, romance is often at the bottom of our priority list. You pencil everything else into your planner. If you can schedule doctor's appointments, hair appointments, and so forth, why not set a few hours aside for each other? Evaluate where you can fit in some quality alone time for you and your significant other – without distracting kids.

The major sleep challenge working mothers are facing right now is having too many obligations and responsibilities. A typical working mom faces another job when she returns home in the evening with cooking, cleaning, baths, homework, and so forth. Many continue working after everyone else has gone to bed.

Moms may have trouble sleeping because of the additional pressure of making ends meet as well as caring for the family. Worrying about finances is traditionally a man's role in two-parent families, but more career moms take on the burden of family finances in addition to bearing the lion's share of home tasks.

Listen to your own body, which will tell you if you're not getting enough daily sleep or rest. Avoid getting to a point where you feel completely burnt out – this may lead to a long-term physical condition or even heart disease or a stroke. Get enough sleep yourself so you can care for your precious loved ones.

Many moms face a lack of time in cooking healthy meals for their families. Yet, what you eat determines your health. Buy seasonal, local produce, which most often is the least expensive and the most nutritious. Create an outline of breakfasts, lunches, and dinners for five days and a corresponding grocery list. Instead of taking trips to the grocery store every other day, do all the shopping in one trip over the weekend. Then, block out several hours to cook four to five meals that you can put in the fridge or freezer for the workweek. Or, cook once, eat twice: cook enough so you can split the food into two meals.

Managing the infant feeding schedule is a common challenge. About the time many mothers return to work after maternity leave (12 weeks), babies are eating about every three to four hours, so if you are working and breastfeeding, try to pump milk every three hours. After four months, rice cereal and solid foods are added to the baby's schedule so it gets easer – feedings may begin to dwindle.

Most moms have to deal with toddler tantrums. When you give in to your toddler, then the toddler learns he or she can get their way by acting in a dramatic way. Consequences of getting his or her way will shape behavior. When a child uses a tantrum to get his or her own way, you need to immediately remove your child to a time-out area.

Every mom has a different childcare selection process. To find the best childcare for your children, reflect on your top needs or goals, educate yourself on the options available, and conduct research to assure yourself that the chosen care is of the utmost quality. There are some alternative lower-cost solutions to childcare centers, like sharing a nanny or babysitter with a close friend to help cut down on cost, while also bringing in social interaction with other children.

Working mothers may feel isolated post-birth, especially if they don't have friends and family close by to help them out. New moms need all the support they can get while caring for babies, feeding on demand, and coping with their own sleep deprivation. Support is also needed beyond a baby's first year.

Technology has made it a bit easier to develop a support network. Check out groups on LinkedIn, Twitter, Facebook, or other social media. Post what you are seeking and see what feedback you get.

Mothers can carve out time for themselves; you must do this for physical and mental health reasons, as well as to be a better parent. It requires sharing family and home obligations with your partner or spouse. Make a schedule every Sunday night, and carve out time in the schedule. Have someone come in and babysit for you even if it's for three hours a week and do a trade if you can't afford it. Swap babysitting with another parent so that each of you has a night off. Get out once a week with your friends, by yourself or with your spouse.

Stuck in a job rut? Follow your career passions. With the huge growth in the availability of flexible jobs over the last several years, working mothers seem to be trading in traditional 9-to-5 workdays in favor of flexible schedules. More employers are offering more flexible options in order to retain this large segment of the workforce.

While today's generation of fathers is expected to be involved in housework and childcare, women often still play the primary role. We expect mothers to be good workers who are highly committed to their work, but they are also the ones held accountable for how their children do and how their households are run.

A June 2011 survey by ForbesWoman and TheBump.com confirmed that most moms resent their partners because they handle far less than their share of the housework and childcare. Most mothers said they feel like single moms, despite being married or living with a partner. This is a sad revelation. Clearly, more fathers have to partake in the housework and become more active in their kids' activities.

How can mothers take their careers to the next level – even with active home lives? Ask your current employer for a change in your schedule – whether that be the option of telecommuting, working flexible hours, working a compressed workweek, or going part-time. Build a solid case for changing your schedule and see if they'd allow some flexibility. If not, then it's time to find a job that does allow flexible work options.

In conclusion, strive to be a good enough mother and not a perfect mother. Perfection is impossible. Do the best you can for your children, yourself, and your partner.

Despite the uncertain economy, don't settle for less than you are worth on the career front. Make sure you are doing work you truly love, and that you are skilled at. Follow your true calling, and you'll reap rewards in due time. Mastering the mommy track is not easy, but you can do it, even in uncertain times.

Visit www.erinflynnjay.com

**BUSINESS
BOOKS**

Business Books encapsulates the freshest thinkers and the most
successful practitioners in the areas of marketing, management,
economics, finance and accounting, sustainable and ethical
business, heart business, people management, leadership,
motivation, biographies, business recovery and development
and personal/executive development.